Get Physical!

An inclusive, therapeutic
PE Programme to develop motor skills

Lois Addy

Every effort has been made to obtain permission for the inclusion in this book of quoted material. Apologies are offered to anyone whom it has not been possible to contact.

Permission to photocopy

This book contains resource sheets which may be reproduced by photocopier or other means for use by the purchaser. This permission is granted on the understanding that these copies will be used within the educational establishment of the purchaser. This book and all its contents remain copyright. Copies may be made without reference to the publisher or to the licensing scheme for the making of photocopies operated by the Publishers' Licensing Agency.

Get Physical!
MT10004
ISBN-13: 978 1 85503 406 8
ISBN-10: 1 85503 406 9
© Lois Addy
Illustrations © Debbie Clark
All rights reserved
First published 2006
Printed in the UK for LDA

Abbeygate House, East Road, Cambridge, CB1 1DB, UK

Contents

Dedication

To my husband Geoff and children, Bethany and Charlotte.

Acknowledgements

I should like to thank the occupational therapists and physiotherapists who were involved in developing and running the Busy Bee (BCB) group in Harrogate for many years, particularly Anita Lindsey, Fran Shipman, Eleanor Jones, Jane Cronin-Davies and Hannah Ives.

I am grateful also to Andy Durrant, School Sport Coordinator for the City of Westminster, for his constructive comments on the first draft of this programme, and to all the teachers who provided valuable feedback on the content and organisation.

Introduction

Promoting engagement in and enthusiasm for physical activity is of increased importance at a time when obesity and low levels of general fitness in the population are causing significant concern, not least among the health professions. All sorts of socio-economic changes have resulted in a generation of children who are not interested in being actively involved in recreational sport, who are less physically active generally – and who are consequently not as fit. The immediate and long-term consequences of leading a sedentary life have been found to be both serious and pervasive. Cardiovascular diseases, obesity, colon cancer, osteoporosis and depression have all been linked to an inactive lifestyle established during youth. In contrast, children who enjoy a high level of physical activity tend to maintain the habit into adulthood, with positive health benefits (Sherman, 2000).

It is therefore vital that there is renewed emphasis on physical education, beginning in the early years with teaching of motor skills that is dynamic, exciting and stimulating. For the teacher, this means providing appropriate activities within a suitable environment – and teaching with enthusiasm and responsiveness. This can be a daunting task because physical ability varies enormously from one child to the next.

An additional concern is how to include children with specific educational needs in the class programme. There are an increasing number of children in mainstream classes who struggle with physical education for a variety of reasons ranging from lack of experience to neurological impairment. This requires the teacher to have a comprehensive understanding of the physical needs of children with diverse abilities, and to accommodate these within a whole-class teaching session. For example, children with Down syndrome will often have low muscle tone resulting in poor stamina; and children with attention-deficit disorder (with or without hyperactivity) may have difficulty coping with the overload of sensory information that arises from simultaneously moving and listening.

Get Physical! is a supplementary physical education scheme that develops the physical skills of *all* children aged 5–7 years at the same time as addressing the needs of children with specific motor coordination difficulties. The programme consists of 40 lesson plans that:

◎ cover the National Curriculum programme of study for games and gymnastics;

◎ provide therapeutic activities to develop important underlying perceptual and motor process skills;

◎ enable children with a variety of special needs to be included in class PE lessons;

◎ are formative and diagnostic, enabling the teacher to identify individual areas of need;

◎ are fun and enjoyable.

The programme relates to the PE National Curriculum for Key Stage 1, covering all areas of knowledge, skills and understanding in the programme of study; and covering games and gymnastics, but *not* dance or the non-statutory area of swimming / water safety. For details of the links, see the programme summary on pages 10–13.

The 40 lesson plans are designed to be easily implemented by non-specialist teachers working within both mainstream and special schools, and may be used with whole classes or with small groups. The programme may also be used outside a class setting by occupational therapists or physiotherapists, or by teachers who want to address the needs of children with specific perceptual–motor or motor learning difficulties on a one-to-one basis or within a small group.

How to use this book

1 Approach and rationale

A brief overview of the underpinning ideas, which will be familiar to therapists but perhaps not so familiar to teachers, is given in Section 1. Detailed knowledge of the rationale is not required for effective delivery of the programme; however, a little background information may be helpful in understanding and addressing the particular needs of some children. Section 1 also includes details of how the programme relates to the PE National Curriculum.

2 Differentiation and assessment

The programme is designed so that every lesson can be differentiated to accommodate and support children with a variety of special educational needs. General strategies for differentiation are given in Section 2; ways to differentiate specific activities are noted in the lesson plans.

As you work through the programme, you have opportunities to observe each child in action. Certain activities may highlight difficulties that are reflected in other aspects of the curriculum. For example, it may become apparent that a child is struggling to remember a sequence of movements, and this same difficulty may be affecting the child's ability to spell or to organise themselves in the classroom. Or it may be apparent that a child cannot accurately assess distances between objects, and this may be affecting their ability to arrange numbers appropriately when doing calculations or to leave spaces between words when writing. Any such areas of difficulty that are identified may be addressed in a variety of ways: through the lessons, through specific classroom activities, or through other programmes such as *Write from the Start* (Teodorescu and Addy, 1996), *Speed Up* (Addy, 2004) or *Brain Gym®* (Dennison, 1992). Advice on the best way to proceed could be sought from a SENCo, physiotherapist, occupational therapist or speech and language therapist.

3 The lesson plans

At the heart of the programme are the lesson plans, found in Section 3. Each lesson plan offers the following:

a clear focus with associated objectives

a list of equipment

a warm-up activity

clear instructions for each activity

a summary of the activities in the lesson

an indication of the approximate timings

National Curriculum objectives and Scottish Guidelines attainment targets

the purpose of each activity – which demonstrates its relationship to the objectives

explanatory diagrams

a cool-down activity

a recap – to reinforce the purpose of the session

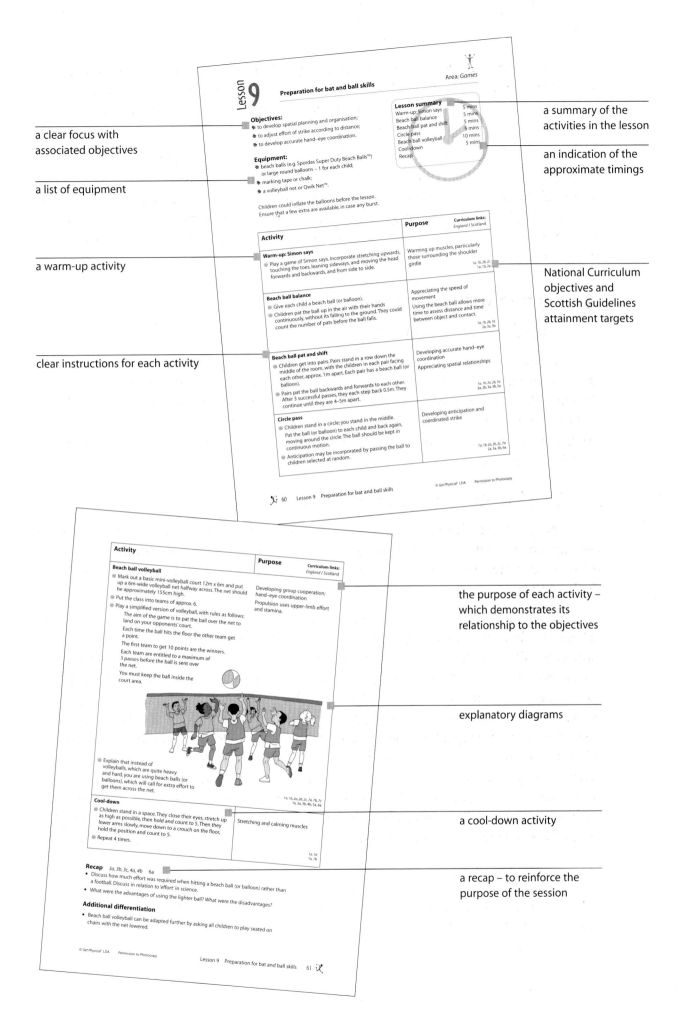

Area: *Games*

Lesson 9

Preparation for bat and ball skills

Objectives:
* to develop spatial planning and organisation;
* to adjust effort of strike according to distance;
* to develop accurate hand–eye coordination.

Equipment:
* beach balls (e.g. Spordas Super Duty Beach Balls™) or large round balloons – 1 for each child;
* marking tape or chalk;
* a volleyball net or Qwik Net™.

Children could inflate the balloons before the lesson. Ensure that a few extra are available, in case any burst.

Lesson summary
Warm-up: Simon says	5 mins
Beach ball balance	5 mins
Beach ball pat and shift	5 mins
Circle pass	5 mins
Beach ball volleyball	10 mins
Cool-down	5 mins
Recap	

Activity	Purpose	Curriculum links: England / Scotland
Warm-up: Simon says ● Play a game of Simon says. Incorporate stretching upwards, touching the toes, leaning sideways, and moving the head forwards and backwards, and from side to side.	Warming up muscles, particularly those surrounding the shoulder girdle	1a, 1b, 2b, 2c 1a, 1b, 2a
Beach ball balance ● Give each child a beach ball (or balloon). ● Children pat the ball up in the air with their hands continuously, without its falling to the ground. They could count the number of pats before the ball falls.	Appreciating the speed of movement Using the beach ball allows more time to assess distance and time between object and contact.	1a, 1b, 2b, 7a 2a, 3a, 3b
Beach ball pat and shift ● Children get into pairs. Pairs stand in a row down the middle of the room, with the children in each pair facing each other, approx. 1m apart. Each pair has a beach ball (or balloon). ● Pairs pat the ball backwards and forwards to each other. After 3 successful passes, they each step back 0.5m. They continue until they are 4–5m apart.	Developing accurate hand–eye coordination Appreciating spatial relationships	1a, 1b, 2a, 2b, 7a 2a, 2b, 3a, 3b, 5a
Circle pass ● Children stand in a circle; you stand in the middle. Pat the ball (or balloon) to each child and back again, moving around the circle. The ball should be kept in continuous motion. ● Anticipation may be incorporated by passing the ball to children selected at random.	Developing anticipation and coordinated strike	1a, 1b, 2a, 2b, 2c, 7a 2a, 3a, 3b, 6a

Activity	Purpose	Curriculum links: England / Scotland
Beach ball volleyball ● Mark out a basic mini-volleyball court 12m x 6m and put up a 6m-wide volleyball net halfway across. The net should be approximately 155cm high. ● Put the class into teams of approx. 6. ● Play a simplified version of volleyball, with rules as follows: The aim of the game is to pat the ball over the net to land on your opponents' court. Each time the ball hits the floor the other team get a point. The first team to get 10 points are the winners. Each team are entitled to a maximum of 3 passes before the ball is sent over the net. You must keep the ball inside the court area. ● Explain that instead of volleyballs, which are quite heavy and hard, you are using beach balls (or balloons), which will call for extra effort to get them across the net.	Developing group cooperation; hand–eye coordination Propulsion uses upper-limb effort and stamina.	1a, 1b, 2a, 2b, 2c, 7a, 7b, 7c 1a, 3a, 3b, 4b, 5a, 6a
Cool-down ● Children stand in a space. They close their eyes, stretch up as high as possible, then hold and count to 5. Then they lower arms slowly, move down to a crouch on the floor, hold the position and count to 5. ● Repeat 4 times.	Stretching and calming muscles	1a, 1b 1a, 1b

Recap   3a, 3b, 3c, 4a, 4b   6a
• Discuss how much effort was required when hitting a beach ball (or balloon) rather than a football. Discuss in relation to 'effort' in science.
• What were the advantages of using the lighter ball? What were the disadvantages?

Additional differentiation
• Beach ball volleyball can be adapted further by asking all children to play seated on chairs with the net lowered.

Each lesson is designed to take between 30 and 45 minutes, depending upon the age and ability of pupils. Lesson plans may be photocopied for easy reference during the lesson.

If the programme is being used outside school in a therapy setting, the therapist could give copies of lesson plans to each child's teacher in order to inform them about the aims, objectives and activities for each session. It would be ideal if the teacher were able to repeat the lesson with the whole class during PE. This would mean that the child receiving the therapy would have an opportunity to repeat and practise activities, and could be called on to demonstrate certain movements or positions from their previous experience – thus promoting self-esteem and self-confidence. Because the programme is aligned with the National Curriculum and develops the skills of all children, the rest of the class would, of course, benefit.

Lesson content and objectives

The focus of the lesson – the main skill that children will be working on – is clearly identified at the top of each lesson plan. This main skill is then broken down into three objectives, the underpinning subskills or 'process skills' that the activities are designed to develop. (See page 16 for more about process skills.) The objectives provide a mix of sensory–motor, psychomotor and affective goals. So movement skills, for example, are balanced with affective goals such as gentle competition, teamwork, cooperation, leadership, assertion, and generation of ideas. In this way, the programme also links to social development and the citizenship curriculum.

It is a good idea to tell children explicitly about the focus of each lesson. Having a clear goal helps them to appreciate how the activities relate to skill acquisition. They are then more likely to engage in the lesson and in subsequent practice outside the classroom. This enhances motor learning as well as self-confidence and self-esteem.

Equipment

None of the activities requires large apparatus or expensive equipment. This means that lessons do not have to be conducted in a specially equipped hall or gym, and could, for example, be done outside. A list of recommended equipment is given for each lesson, and low-cost alternatives are suggested wherever possible.

The activities

Each lesson begins with a warm-up activity. This is a game or exercise to warm up the muscles gently so they are ready for more vigorous movement. If vigorous movement is attempted when the body is not warmed up, the muscles will be stiffer and movement more limited. There is also an increased risk of strain or injury. It is therefore important that every child joins in the warm-up activities. Children will, of course, become quickly bored with the same or similar warm-up exercises, so the programme uses a variety of warm-ups.

The warm-up is followed by the introduction of the key skill. This might be a foundation skill or a specific task. A series of large- or small-group games incorporates the focus skill. Some of these include an element of competition, and this can be either hyped up or omitted, according to the needs and abilities of the children.

The lesson concludes with a short cool-down activity to reduce the pace in preparation for the concluding discussion.

The recap

It is recommended that each session ends with a discussion that provides an opportunity to share positive feedback and for children to reflect openly on the lesson aims and objectives.

The suggested discussion topics will reinforce the purpose of the session and explain the benefits in terms of health and fitness. Children can discuss how the body moves, how the skill may be utilised elsewhere, how the skill may be expanded and how skills could be practised. The recap also provides an opportunity to link the lesson with other aspects of the curriculum; for example movement sequences which incorporate alterations in height can be linked to the estimation and assessment of height differences in mathematics.

The recap can follow straight on from the activities while the children are still in the hall, gym or wherever. Alternatively, it could be done after returning to the classroom.

Fun

Many of the activities used in the programme incorporate humour and fun: this is an important motivator for children. There is also scope for introducing an element of competition into some activities. You should use this with discretion in order to boost the self-confidence and self-esteem of those in the group.

The **programme summary** on pages 10–13 shows which underlying skills are covered in each lesson. If you feel a child or group would benefit from working on a particular skill or set of skills, you can use the programme summary to find the lesson or lessons to use.

Finally, the **motor skills checklist** on pages 35–36 can be used to monitor children's progress and as a reminder of the motor skills which children should have acquired by the end of Key Stage 1.

Programme summary

Lesson no.	Aim	Objectives	National Curriculum objectives / Scottish Guidelines attainment targets
1	**Observation and listening skills**	◎ to develop concentration and listening skills, stressing their importance when developing movement skills; ◎ to develop group cooperation; ◎ to encourage observation and attention.	*1a, 1b, 2a, 2b, 2c, 3a, 3b, 3c, 4a, 4b, 6b, 7a* 1a, 2b, 3a, 3b, 4a, 4b, 5a, 5b, 6a
2	**Ball propulsion (push)**	◎ to develop hip-girdle stability and flexibility; ◎ to control low-level ball propulsion; ◎ to increase shoulder strength and control.	*1a, 1b, 2a, 2b, 2c, 3a, 3b, 3c, 4a, 4b, 7a, 7b, 7c* 1a, 1b, 2a, 2b, 3a, 3b, 4a, 5a, 6a
3	**Accurate throw 1**	◎ to develop hand–eye coordination; ◎ to develop propulsion skills; ◎ to assess spatial relationships.	*1a, 1b, 2a, 2b, 2c, 3a, 3b, 3c, 4a, 4b, 7a, 7b, 7c* 1a, 1b, 2a, 2b, 3a, 3b, 4b, 5a, 6a
4	**Accurate throw 2**	◎ to throw a ball at a target; ◎ to assess the speed and direction of a ball; ◎ to accommodate spatial planning and organisation.	*1a, 1b, 2a, 2b, 2c, 3a, 3b, 3c, 4a, 4b, 7a, 7b, 7c* 1a, 1b, 2a, 2b, 3a, 3b, 4b, 5a, 6a
5	**Catch**	◎ to develop bilateral coordination; ◎ to extend hand–eye coordination; ◎ to expand motor planning and organisation skills.	*1a, 1b, 2b, 2c, 3a, 3b, 3c, 4a, 4b, 7a, 7b, 7c* 1a, 1b, 2a, 2b, 3a, 3b, 4b, 5a, 5b, 6a
6	**Throw and catch 1**	◎ to develop the ability to send and receive an object accurately; ◎ to assess response to form constancy (speed to accommodate different-sized objects); ◎ to develop tactics for avoidance and interception.	*1a, 1b, 2b, 2c, 3a, 3b, 3c, 4a, 4b, 7a, 7b, 7c* 1a, 1b, 2a, 2b, 3a, 3b, 4a, 4b, 5a, 6a
7	**Throw and catch 2**	◎ to develop shoulder-girdle stability; ◎ to develop accurate targeting skills; ◎ to encourage accurate catch by using a slower-moving object.	*1a, 1b, 2a, 2b, 2c, 3a, 3b, 3c, 4a, 4b, 7a, 7b, 7c* 1a, 2a, 2b, 3a, 3b, 4b, 5a, 6a
8	**Alternative methods of throwing and catching**	◎ to develop ball projection; ◎ to develop team cooperation; ◎ to self-regulate upper-limb effort.	*1a, 1b, 2a, 2b, 2c, 3a, 3b, 3c, 4a, 4b, 7a, 7b, 8a* 1a, 1b, 2a, 2b, 3a, 3b, 4a, 4b, 5a, 5b, 6a
9	**Preparation for bat and ball skills**	◎ to develop spatial planning and organisation; ◎ to adjust effort of strike according to distance; ◎ to develop accurate hand–eye coordination.	*1a, 1b, 2a, 2b, 2c, 3a, 3b, 3c, 4a, 4b, 7a, 7b, 7c* 1a, 1b, 2a, 2b, 3a, 3b, 4b, 5a, 6a
10	**Bat and ball skills 1**	◎ to develop successful hand–eye coordination; ◎ to encourage accurate assessment of space and speed; ◎ to develop effective strike action.	*1a, 1b, 2a, 2b, 2c, 3a, 3b, 3c, 4a, 4b, 6b, 7a, 7b, 7c* 1a, 1b, 2a, 2b, 3a, 3b, 4b, 4c, 5a, 5b, 6a

Lesson no.	Aim	Objectives	National Curriculum objectives / Scottish Guidelines attainment targets
11	**Bat and ball skills 2**	◎ to develop hand–eye coordination; ◎ to encourage accurate assessment of space and speed; ◎ to improve response times.	*1a, 1b, 2b, 2c, 3a, 3b, 3c, 4a, 4b, 7a, 7b, 7c* 1a, 1b, 2a, 2b, 3a, 3b, 3c, 4a, 4b, 4c, 5a, 5b, 6a
12	**Bat and ball skills 3**	◎ to develop laterality; ◎ to encourage crossing of the body's midline; ◎ to expand bilateral hand–eye coordination.	*1a, 1b, 2a, 2b, 2c, 3a, 3b, 3c, 4a, 4b, 7a, 7b, 7c* 1a, 1b, 2a, 2b, 3a, 3b, 4a, 4b, 4c, 5a, 5b, 6a
13	**Object transfer 1**	◎ to develop bimanual coordination; ◎ to develop midline orientation; ◎ to extend shoulder-girdle stability.	*1a, 1b, 2a, 2b, 2c, 3b, 3c, 4a, 4b, 7a, 7b* 1a, 1b, 2a, 2b, 3a, 3b, 4b, 5a, 5b, 6a
14	**Object transfer 2**	◎ to encourage pressure through the upper limbs; ◎ to develop bilateral control and reciprocal action; ◎ to increase shoulder strength.	*1a, 1b, 2a, 2b, 3a, 3b, 3c, 4a, 4b, 7a, 7b* 1a, 1b, 2a, 2b, 3a, 3b, 4b, 4c, 5a, 6a
15	**Object transfer 3**	◎ to develop cooperation and teamwork; ◎ to enhance motor planning and organisation; ◎ to create alternative motor strategies.	*1a, 1b, 2a, 2b, 2c, 3a, 3b, 3c, 4a, 4b, 7a, 7b, 7c* 1a, 1b, 2a, 2b, 3a, 3b, 4a, 4b, 5a, 5b, 6a
16	**Controlled kick 1**	◎ to develop cooperative teamwork; ◎ to enhance joint position sense (proprioception) by increasing effort through the upper and lower limbs; ◎ to increase tactile sensation and therefore enhance self-awareness (body schema).	*1a, 1b, 2a, 2b, 2c, 3a, 3b, 3c, 4a, 4b, 7b, 7c* 1a, 1b, 2a, 3a, 3b, 4a, 4b, 5a, 5b, 6a
17	**Controlled kick 2**	◎ to develop stability of the hip and shoulder girdle; ◎ to enhance strength in upper limbs; ◎ to explore new ways of moving in space.	*1a, 1b, 2a, 2b, 2c, 3a, 3b, 3c, 4a, 4b, 7a, 7b, 7c, 8a* 1a, 1b, 2a, 2b, 3a, 3b, 4c, 5a, 5b, 6a
18	**Accurate kick**	◎ to develop controlled foot–eye coordination; ◎ to encourage accurate spatial assessment and organisation; ◎ to develop accurate foot-strike action.	*1a, 1b, 2a, 2b, 2c, 3a, 3b, 3c, 4a, 4b, 7a, 7b, 7c* 1a, 1b, 2a, 2b, 3a, 3b, 4c, 5a, 5b, 6a
19	**Observation and invasion games 1**	◎ to encourage rapid assessment of space needed when playing invasion games; ◎ to enhance visual figure–ground discrimination; ◎ to develop group tactics.	*1a, 1b, 2a, 2b, 2c, 3a, 3b, 3c, 4a, 4b, 6b, 7a, 7b, 7c* 1a, 1b, 2a, 2b, 3a, 3b, 4b, 5a, 5b, 6a
20	**Observation and invasion games 2**	◎ to develop observation skills; ◎ to enhance body awareness and body schema; ◎ to develop controlled movement.	*1a, 1b, 2a, 2b, 2c, 3a, 3b, 3c, 4a, 4b, 7a, 7c, 8a* 1a, 2a, 2b, 3a, 3b, 4a, 4b, 5a, 5b, 6a
21	**Observation and listening skills**	◎ to develop listening skills; ◎ to develop sequential memory; ◎ to enhance motor skills and coordination.	*1a, 1b, 2a, 2b, 2c, 3a, 3b, 3c, 4a, 4b, 8a, 8b* 1a, 1b, 2a, 2b, 3a, 3b, 4b, 5a, 5b, 6a

Lesson no.	Aim	Objectives	National Curriculum objectives Scottish Guidelines attainment targets
22	Movement in space 1	◎ to develop spatial awareness; ◎ to assess distance and location within a mobile environment; ◎ to develop coordinated movement.	*1a, 1b, 2a, 2b, 2c, 3a, 3b, 3c, 4a, 4b, 8a, 8b, 8c* 1a, 2a, 2b, 3a, 3b, 4b, 4c, 5a, 5b, 6a
23	Movement in space 2	◎ to encourage spatial perception during movement; ◎ to develop spatial awareness with simultaneous observation skills; ◎ to develop balance and body awareness.	*1a, 1b, 2a, 2b, 2c, 3a, 3b, 3c, 4a, 4b, 8a, 8b, 8d* 1a, 1b, 2a, 2b, 3a, 3b, 4b, 5a, 5b, 6a
24	Four-point balance	◎ to develop hip and shoulder stability; ◎ to develop increased stamina while balancing; ◎ to develop reciprocal movements.	*1a, 1b, 2a, 2b, 2c, 3a, 3b, 3c, 4a, 4b, 8a, 8b, 8c, 8d* 1a, 1b, 2a, 2b, 3a, 3b, 4a, 4b, 4c, 5a, 5b, 6a
25	Balance on alternate legs 1	◎ to balance on either leg; ◎ to develop static and dynamic balance; ◎ to appreciate why this skill is necessary.	*1a, 1b, 2a, 2b, 2c, 3a, 3b, 3c, 4a, 4b, 8a, 8b, 8c, 8d* 1a, 1b, 2a, 2b, 3a, 3b, 4a, 4b, 5a, 5b, 6a
26	Balance on alternate legs 2	◎ to reinforce skills introduced in previous lesson; ◎ to extend ability to balance on alternate legs; ◎ to improve balance and motion skills.	*1a, 1b, 2a, 2b, 2c, 3a, 3b, 3c, 4a, 4b, 8a, 8b, 8d* 1a, 1b, 2a, 2b, 3a, 3b, 4a, 4b, 5a, 6a
27	One-leg balance	◎ to develop unilateral balance skills; ◎ to develop motor organisation and planning; ◎ to enhance spatial awareness.	*1a, 1b, 2a, 2b, 2c, 3a, 3b, 3c, 4a, 4b, 6a, 8a, 8b, 8c* 1a, 1b, 2a, 2b, 3a, 3b, 4b, 5a, 5b, 6a
28	One-leg balance with resistance	◎ to maintain balance against resistance; ◎ to develop both static and dynamic balance; ◎ to extend proprioception and kinaesthetic sense.	*1a, 1b, 2a, 2b, 2c, 3a, 3b, 3c, 4a, 4b, 8a, 8b* 1a, 1b, 2a, 2b, 3a, 4b, 5a, 5b, 6a
29	Upper-limb coordination 1	◎ to develop shoulder-girdle stability; ◎ to increase strength in shoulder girdle; ◎ to enhance upper-limb proprioception.	*1a, 1b, 2a, 2b, 2c, 3a, 3b, 3c, 4a, 4b, 8a, 8b, 8c* 1a, 1b, 2a, 2b, 3a, 3b, 4a, 5a, 5b, 6a
30	Upper-limb coordination 2	◎ to develop strength in the shoulder girdle; ◎ to encourage weight bearing through the shoulders; ◎ to provide proprioceptive feedback through extended arms.	*1a, 1b, 2a, 2b, 2c, 3a, 3b, 3c, 4a, 4b, 8a, 8b, 8c* 1a, 1b, 2a, 2b, 3b, 4b, 5a, 5b, 6a
31	Resistance – push	◎ to enhance awareness of deep pressure through the upper and lower limbs; ◎ to increase strength in upper and lower limbs; ◎ to maintain postural control against resistance.	*1a, 1b, 2b, 2c, 3a, 3b, 3c, 4a, 4b, 8a, 8b* 1b, 2a, 2b, 3a, 3b, 5a, 6a
32	Resistance – pull	◎ to develop strength in upper limbs; ◎ to stimulate deep muscle sensation to improve motor control; ◎ to enjoy simple team games incorporating pulling activities.	*1a, 1b, 2a, 2b, 2c, 3a, 3b, 3c, 4a, 4b, 8a, 8b, 8c, 8d* 1a, 1b, 2a, 2b, 3a, 3b, 4a, 4b, 5a, 5b, 6a

Lesson no.	Aim	Objectives	National Curriculum objectives / Scottish Guidelines attainment targets
33	**Body awareness 1**	◎ to enhance body awareness by stimulating touch receptors; ◎ to improve motor coordination by increasing the awareness of limb position; ◎ to increase observation skills in order to refine motor control.	*1a, 1b, 2a, 2b, 2c, 3a, 3b, 3c, 4a, 4b, 8b, 8c* 1a, 1b, 2a, 2b, 3a, 3b, 4a, 4b, 4c, 5a, 5b, 6a
34	**Body awareness 2**	◎ to develop an awareness of how the body moves; ◎ to develop motor control and balance; ◎ to develop an accurate body image.	*1a, 1b, 2a, 2b, 2c, 3a, 3b, 3c, 4a, 4b, 8b* 2a, 3a, 3b, 4a, 4b, 4c, 5a, 5b, 6a
35	**Action sequences 1**	◎ to develop acute observation skills; ◎ to memorise sequences of movements; ◎ to make timely movements.	*1a, 1b, 2a, 2b, 2c, 3a, 3b, 3c, 4a, 4b, 8b, 8c, 8d* 1a, 1b, 2a, 3a, 3b, 4a, 4b, 5a, 5b, 6a
36	**Action sequences 2**	◎ to develop sequential memory; ◎ to provide cues to help aid recall; ◎ to develop spatial planning and organisation.	*1a, 1b, 2a, 2b, 2c, 3a, 3b, 3c, 4a, 4b, 8a, 8b, 8d* 1a, 2a, 3a, 3b, 5a, 5b, 6a
37	**Assessment of space 1**	◎ to develop spatial planning and organisation; ◎ to develop coordinated movements; ◎ to develop assessment and approximation.	*1a, 1b, 2a, 2b, 2c, 3a, 3b, 3c, 4a, 4b, 8a, 8b* 1a, 2a, 2b, 3a, 3b, 4a, 4b, 5a, 5b, 6a
38	**Assessment of space 2**	◎ to develop spatial planning; ◎ to observe individual ability to judge distances at speed; ◎ to increase motor-response time.	*1a, 1b, 2a, 2b, 2c, 3a, 3b, 3c, 4a, 4b, 8a, 8b, 8c* 1a, 1b, 2a, 2b, 3a, 3b, 4a, 4b, 5a, 6a
39	**Assessment of space 3**	◎ to develop spatial organisation; ◎ to increase tactile sensation which enhances body image; ◎ to develop group cooperation and teamwork.	*1a, 1b, 2a, 2b, 2c, 3a, 3b, 3c, 4a, 4b, 8a, 8b, 8c* 1a, 2a, 2b, 3a, 3b, 4b, 4c, 5a, 6a
40	**Rolling and turning**	◎ to apply deep pressure to stimulate kinaesthetic sense and heighten body schema; ◎ to apply effort through the hips and trunk in order to promote movement; ◎ to develop controlled rolling in a variety of directions and planes.	*1a, 1b, 2a, 2b, 2c, 3a, 3b, 3c, 4a, 4b, 8a, 8b, 8d* 1a, 2a, 2b, 3a, 3b, 4a, 4b, 5a, 5b, 6a

1 Approach and rationale 𝓕

𝓕 The development of the programme

The *Get Physical!* programme has been devised by a paediatric occupational therapist with over 23 years' experience of working with children with a variety of special educational needs (SEN), in both mainstream and special schools, and in clinic and community settings. This work – which predominantly addressed perceptual and motor needs of children – has provided the basis for an analysis of children's movement skills and the development of a systematic programme for teaching motor concepts and processes.

Get Physical! has its origins in an after-school programme developed for children aged between 4 and 11 years with motor learning difficulties. As the inclusion of children with SEN in mainstream schools prevailed, it was further developed for use within both health and educational settings.

The programme was developed in collaboration with other occupational therapists as well as physiotherapists and teachers. On reviewing the objectives of the different professionals working in this situation, it became apparent that the expectations of teacher and therapist did not differ greatly. Any differences tended to be in relation to terminology and professional bias. If we take objective 7a in the PE National Curriculum programme of study at Key Stage 1, for example, and compare it with the skills required from an occupational therapy or physiotherapy perspective, we can see that the goals are roughly the same; what differs is the terminology used and how that goal is achieved.

National Curriculum objective	Skills required from a therapeutic perspective	
Pupils should be taught to: a. Travel with,	*Skills to travel:* Reciprocal motor patterning to move Ability to initiate movement Ability to stop movement without 'overflow' Rhythmicity of movement	
send …	*Skills to throw an object:* Hand–eye coordination Ability to assess space Appreciation of spatial relationships	Rhythmic coordination Bimanual skills including bilateral integration
and receive a ball and other equipment in different ways	*Skills to receive an object:* Rapid assessment of spatial relationships Speed of motor planning	Motor organisation Figure–ground discrimination Intact form and size constancy

Both therapy directives and educational objectives are therefore combined in the *Get Physical!* programme to enhance the motor skills of all children – including those with specific motor difficulties.

The acquisition of skills
A dual approach

In the course of teaching efficient motor planning and motor execution, two specific approaches are used: a process-orientated (or general abilities) approach, and a task-centred (or specific skills) approach. There is ongoing debate about which approach is more effective, but each one has its place when working with children aged 5 to 7 years – and *Get Physical!* incorporates them both. Over the course of the programme, both perceptual and kinaesthetic activities and specific skill-based sessions are included.

A process-orientated approach

The programme is based on the premise that fundamental motor skills form the building blocks from which more advanced and complex movements or skills can be 'constructed'. The carefully structured teaching of the foundation skills helps children control their bodies, manipulate their environment and acquire complex movement patterns which will ultimately provide the basis for enjoyment of sport and other recreational activities (Payne and Isaacs, 2002).

Get Physical! incorporates a 'bottom-up' or process-orientated approach, and is structured around activities based on principles of **sensory–motor** development, **kinaesthetic** regulation and **perceptual–motor** training. This essentially psychological approach is based on identifying the underlying processes involved in acquiring a specific skill, and then developing these process skills to provide the foundation on which other skills are built.

So, for example, if the target skill is to catch a ball, the following process skills would be needed:

- midline orientation (bringing the hands to the midline of the body);
- bilateral integration (simultaneous use of both hands);
- visual–spatial assessment;
- temporal awareness (appreciation of speed and timing);
- form constancy (appreciation of the size of the ball);
- proprioception (awareness of the limbs' position).

Intervention consists of facilitation of balance and physical abilities, and perceptual–motor tasks.

Perceptual–motor training

Perceptual–motor training is one method which uses a process-orientated approach. In order to hit a ball with a racket, for example, perceptual skills such as hand–eye coordination, visual–spatial planning and size constancy all need to be intact in order to assess the size of the ball and the distance of the ball from the bat. In addition, before the ball can be hit successfully, kinaesthetic sensation and vestibular regulation are needed to position the body in relation to the bat and ball, to engage the correct motor patterns and to assess the speed of the ball. The supposition is that by enhancing these underpinning skills, both this action and other actions requiring these skills will be advanced. For example, by focusing on activities relating to spatial planning tasks, such as obstacle courses, the child will also show improvements in spatial organisation in other areas such as science, handwriting and art.

We know that processes such as perception are not innately fixed and continue to develop and adapt with age, experience and instruction. Children aged between 4 and 8 years seem particularly receptive to perceptual and motor learning, in particular in relation to depth perception and form discrimination (Addy, 1995; Addy, 1996; Schoemaker *et al.*, 1994). This is why the programme includes activities to develop these areas.

Kinaesthetic training

Kinaesthetic training is another process-orientated approach. The evidence supporting the use of pure kinaesthetic training is somewhat controversial. Research by Laszlo and Bairstow (1985), who designed kinaesthetic training programmes to develop kinaesthetic acuity and memory, has been questioned by those who have replicated this approach with less significant results (Sims *et al.*, 1996; Polatajko *et al.*, 1995). However, they did concur that the improvements seen using this approach were 'as good as other methods of motor-skill training'. One criticism of kinaesthetic training is that it requires the child to reproduce passive movement; another is that it does not use 'real-life' actions. Kinaesthetic activities are included in the *Get Physical!* programme, but in a way that requires active engagement by children. Moreover, the activities are context based, which is an essential condition for successful motor-skill acquisition (Van der Weel *et al.*, 1991).

Developing process skills through the programme

Approximately half of the activities incorporated into the *Get Physical!* programme enhance the prerequisite process skills in preparation for acquiring more complex skills. Lesson 7, for example, focuses entirely on activities to increase shoulder-girdle stability – which is a vital prerequisite for many motor tasks such as handwriting, cutting with scissors, and ball catching and throwing. It is also necessary for many gymnastic skills such as four-point balances, forward rolls, handstands, cartwheels and vault work.

There may be several children in a class who, for one reason or another, have not acquired these process skills. In this programme, the skills are introduced in very simple ways, with tasks gradually increasing in complexity in order to ensure success and maintain confidence and motivation.

A task-centred approach

The physical task-centred approach involves teaching a specific skill without emphasising the underlying processes, and is the approach taken by most physical education training (Sugden and Wright, 1998). The skill is subdivided, instructed and rehearsed until it has been mastered. This is particularly useful in learning a complex skill which has been selected by the child; whereas children may struggle to see the relevance of certain perceptual or sensory activities, they are likely to be motivated to acquire a skill for which they can see a use. However, it could also be argued that very young children are not really able to identify skills they would like to acquire. In addition, for this approach to work, the activity must be practised in various contexts several times each week, and there is limited time available in the curriculum for PE – which is typically included once or twice a week.

The activities in the programme therefore incorporate skills which enable most young children to succeed in common playground games such as hopscotch, skipping, football, other ball games, hoopla and french skipping.

Get Physical! incorporates such a top-down or task-centred approach, but the programme is carefully structured so that a lesson focusing on a specific skill is preceded by lessons designed to develop the underpinning processes for that skill. For example, strike (kick) skills are preceded by lessons focusing on unilateral balance. The task-specific activities use demonstration, participation, feedback, rehearsal and practice to reinforce skill acquisition. This ensures that children acquire key skills that are required for sporting activities – for example, certain ball skills such as upper-limb ball strike need to be developed before rounders or baseball is introduced.

The programme summary (on pages 10–13) will help you to pinpoint lessons that address particular skill areas. In addition, the variation in lesson themes should maintain the motivation of pupils and encourage practice outside the PE lesson, which in turn will ensure that skills are established and refined. The incorporation of variable practice into the child's school day will encourage generalisation of skills.

Motor processes

There are two key processes which influence the successful acquisition of motor skills: motor preparation and motor execution. Both are specifically targeted by *Get Physical!* programme activities.

Motor preparation

For any specific action, adequate motor preparation is essential for success. This involves selecting the correct starting position, assessing environmental variables, organising and selecting previous movement patterns from memory, comprehending the anticipated action, and predicting the energy and effort required to initiate the movement. Once we have become proficient in an action, this becomes an entirely subconscious process. However, when we attempt a new type of action, initially we have to engage motor preparation processes at a more conscious level. This requires intact **kinaesthesia**.

Kinaesthesia

Kinaesthesia is the perception of the body's position, movement and muscular tension. Receptors located in our joints provide us with a mental image or map of the exact position of our limbs in relation to our body; other receptors located in our tendons and muscles indicate how much we have moved. Thus, kinaesthesia enables us to refine both fine and gross motor skills. It also allows us to perform actions without relying on vision – as when we brush the hair at the back of our head or tie apron strings.

In addition to kinaesthesia, vision plays a central role in achieving balance during the first three years of life. Children under the age of 3 are very dependent on vision to help their motor control. Their desperate need to see in order to understand and make sense of their environment is the reason why they find it impossible to play blindfold games. As children mature, they begin to use other forms of sensory information and, in particular, their kinaesthetic sense to extend their motor skills. This weaning off reliance on visual cues continues up to the age of about 10. However, there are those who continue this visual dependence and, as a consequence, are unable to activate several actions at once. This is particularly true of children with a **developmental coordination disorder** (DCD).

You can observe whether a child is reluctant to use their kinaesthetic sense in the following way. Ask the child to stand upright with their eyes closed for 60 seconds. Increased postural sway will be noted amongst those who rely on vision rather than other forms of sensory information to guide their movements.

Get Physical! incorporates several activities where the kinaesthetic sense is stimulated to reduce the need to rely on vision. For example, lesson 31 includes wall press-ups, pushing, and resistance activities, all of which apply pressure through the receptors in the muscles and joints to indicate their exact position, which helps with motor control.

The vestibular system in the inner ear is also involved in motor planning. It acts as a regulator, helping to maintain balance in sitting, standing and moving, as well as detecting the speed and direction of movements. Slight distortions in this system may produce nausea, vertigo and dizziness, and may result in a lack of coordinated movement. Accurate kinaesthetic feedback, together with information processed through the vestibular system, helps to facilitate balance. It is important to notice if any child appears to have difficulty in maintaining an upright position or in adjusting to changes in direction. Ask children to run around the room at various speeds and in various directions. Observe whether any child appears uncomfortable when moving at speed. Does the same child prefer to perform activities from the floor? Does the child struggle to change direction on command? If so, this may indicate difficulties in balance and accommodating speed of movement. It is important for all children to be able to alter movements on command, so activities involving sudden changes are included. You could provide a 'secret cue' to help children who struggle with an instantaneous response – for example, you could clap three times before an instruction is given, allowing children time to stop an action in anticipation for the command.

The combination of the kinaesthetic and the vestibular senses together with other sensory information – from touch, vision, hearing, taste and smell – provides the basis for developing perception. This provides additional information relating to the individual and the environment.

Perception

Perception can be defined as an awareness or representation of something via the senses. Aspects of perception include the development of **hand–eye coordination, form/shape constancy, figure–ground discrimination, awareness of position in space, spatial relationships** and **visual closure**. Each aspect of perception provides the child with further information which can be utilised in the successful planning of movements. For example, vision helps to assess and accommodate the environment and location of objects in relation to self and each other; this visual sequential assessment of space provides a mental map which tells us where movement can successfully take place.

Perceptual development begins early in life, with the child acquiring the ability to recognise objects and appreciate their permanence at 7 months of age, and continues up to the age of 7 years. It is therefore appropriate that the various aspects of perception should be encouraged, expanded and integrated alongside children's motor performance.

Perception may be distorted in children who are not receiving accurate information through their kinaesthetic or sensory system. If this is the case, then errors will be seen in positioning, judgement of space, and assessment of speed and velocity. Amongst the lessons there are several activities that will aid perceptual development – and that will allow you to observe this aspect of children's abilities.

Language

In addition to activating the appropriate movement mechanisms required to achieve successful movement, children need to understand what it is they are expected to do. This involves an appreciation of movement concepts, spatial concepts and laterality. The English language is complex, and several verbs can be used to describe the same concept. The PE lesson provides an opportunity to introduce movement terminology which can be reinforced with actions and demonstration. For example, lessons 33 and 34 incorporate games which refer to specific movement and spatial concepts.

Movement execution

This follows the planning phase and involves the activation of movement patterns. As with movement planning, it involves the coordination of several systems – for example, when we reach down to pick up an object such as a beanbag, key muscles are activated to help us to lean forward and to stretch our arm forward and downward. At the same time, anticipatory muscles respond by maintaining balance so that we do not topple over. Some children – with or without an identifiable condition – may struggle to activate these anticipatory movements, causing actions to slow down. You may notice a delay in response from these children, who appear clumsy and slow in their movements. To accommodate these needs, the programme carefully grades certain movements so that adjustments can be made, rehearsed and then extended. In this way, it encourages successful movement rather than risking potential failure because a task has placed too great a demand on the child's ability.

Movement action may also be affected by speed of information processing. Children with language and/or learning difficulties may struggle with the speed of processing patterns of movements, and therefore may require more basic 'safe' movements in order to have more time to accommodate movements needed to assist in balance.

Cognitive processes

In addition to the physical motor systems required for successful motor coordination, cognitive processes such as memory and attention are also required. Children with attention-deficit/hyperactivity disorder (ADHD) have particular problems 'doing' and 'listening' simultaneously, so they are quick to go off task or 'do their own thing'. For this reason it is important to double-check that the child has followed the instructions and knows exactly what is expected. Verbal rehearsal together with an action will aid recall.

Excessive auditory stimuli may prove a distraction for children with ADHD, and a busy, echoing hall or gym is a far from quiet environment. It is for this reason that many activities control space and movement, thus limiting the overload of both visual and auditory information.

Limited physical experience

Physical experience may be limited in children whose movements are restricted by abnormal muscle tone. For example, a child with cerebral palsy may not know what it is like to extend (straighten) their arms. When giving a command such as 'Place your straight arms out to the side', a physical prompt may be needed to help the child to 'feel' what it is like to have 'straight' arms. This is also true for children with a poor body schema, such as those with DCD, Williams syndrome or anorexia.

The *Get Physical!* programme aims to develop both motor preparation and motor execution in all pupils, so that they can enjoy movement and physical activity. This may mean that specific targets are set for children who struggle to acquire these motor skills. These can be determined by the teacher, in collaboration with the child and their physiotherapist or occupational therapist, and included in the child's individual education plan (IEP). Higher expectations can be set for those who are more able. The teacher's ability to adjust the demands of each activity is therefore very important.

Get Physical! and the National Curriculum

Get Physical! is aligned with the National Curriculum for England and Wales. It may also be adapted to comply with the Common Curriculum for Northern Ireland (1989), the 5–14 Guidelines for Scotland (2000), or with any other programme.

The table below shows how the programme relates to the National Curriculum for England and Wales.

National Curriculum	Get Physical!
Knowledge, skills and understanding	
1 Acquiring and developing skills	
Pupils should be taught to:	
• explore basic skills, actions and ideas with increasing understanding • remember and repeat simple skills and actions with increasing control and coordination	*In each lesson, activities start very simply and gradually progress to quite complex games. Repetition and rehearsal contribute to skill improvement and generalisation; warm-up activities are nevertheless varied throughout the programme to maintain enthusiasm and enjoyment.*
2 Selecting and applying skills, tactics and compositional ideas	
Pupils should be taught to:	
• explore how to choose and apply skills and actions in sequence and in combination • vary the way they perform skills by using simple tactics and movement phrases • apply rules and conventions for different activities	*Although the programme is highly structured and directive, there are ample opportunities for children to develop ideas and imagination. The extension and application of ideas is explored during the recap session, and practice at other times is encouraged.*
3 Evaluating and improving performance	
Pupils should be taught to:	
• describe what they have done • observe, describe and copy what others have done • use what they have learnt to improve the quality and control of their work	*Again the focus of the recap session is on evaluating the lesson and discussing its applicability to other aspects of the curriculum.*

National Curriculum	Get Physical!

4 Knowledge and understanding of fitness and health

Pupils should be taught:

- how important it is to be active
- to recognise and describe how their bodies feel during different activities

There is a clear set of aims and objectives for each activity, which can be imparted to the children. This will encourage real engagement rather than simple compliance. This engagement is dynamic and involves commitment, effort and motivation to master relevant skills through rehearsal and practice.

Breadth of study

5

During the key stage, pupils should be taught the knowledge, skills and understanding through dance activities, games activities and gymnastic activities.

The programme focuses specifically on two areas: games and gymnastics, with lesson plans being divided equally between the two.

7 Games activities

Pupils should be taught to:

- travel with, send and receive a ball and other equipment in different ways
- develop these skills for simple net, striking/fielding and invasion-type games
- play simple, competitive net, striking/fielding and invasion-type games that they and others have made, using simple tactics for attacking and defending.

Twenty lesson plans relate to this section of the curriculum, although many of the activities may seem somewhat unconventional and may use some unusual equipment. This is deliberate, so that the children can learn to adapt traditional games in order to explore new skills, and not be restricted by lack of sports equipment.

Inexpensive materials can be adapted to create scoops, bats, mats, targets, and so on.

8 Gymnastic activities

Pupils should be taught to:

- perform basic skills in travelling, being still, finding space and using it safely, both on the floor and using apparatus
- develop the range of their skills and actions [for example, balancing, taking off and landing, turning and rolling]
- choose and link skills and actions in short movement phrases
- create and perform short, linked sequences that show a clear beginning, middle and end and have contrasts in direction, level and speed.

Twenty lesson plans include activities which focus on these directives, although these are presented as a series of challenging games rather than the type of activity generally thought of as traditional gymnastics.

In addition, the National Curriculum recommends that 'teaching should ensure that when evaluating and improving performance, connections are made between developing, selecting and applying skills, tactics and compositional ideas, and fitness and health'. Positive comments and feedback from the recap sessions should assist in helping children to debate how skills can be applied and practised outside the PE lesson.

Links to the National Curriculum for England and Wales and to the Scottish National Guidelines are given for each lesson in the programme summary on pages 10–13 and for each activity as it appears on the lesson plan.

Differentiation and evaluation

All children have different abilities, so a differentiated curriculum is relevant not only to those with an identified SEN but to all those in a particular class. Of course, it is not necessarily appropriate or possible to provide each child with an individualised programme. Nevertheless, the *Get Physical!* lesson plans offer activities and games which can be easily adapted or modified to ensure that all individuals have an opportunity to participate and to extend their skills and abilities within every lesson. This is achieved by having a core lesson which is sufficiently structured and graded to introduce and extend skills gradually, and flexible enough to include adaptations and modifications introduced at the teacher's discretion.

Black and Haskins (1996) suggest there are three ways in which a PE lesson can be differentiated. Firstly, teachers can offer parallel activities where all children play the same game, but each in their own way. For example, children may be encouraged to run around the room, changing directions on command. This may not be possible for children with cerebral palsy because of restricted mobility, but they may be able to crawl around the room and respond according to the teacher's commands.

Secondly, there are occasions when it is important and appropriate to adapt a game or activity, for example seated volleyball or floor football. The *Get Physical!* programme incorporates many such adapted activities. This may give rise to concern that the lessons are not conventional PE units of work. However, even though some games may seem unorthodox, they are guaranteed to develop underlying motor control and coordination skills. Similarly, there may be concern that activities adapted for children with SEN may restrict the abilities of more able children. There is no reason for this to happen, especially if expectations of more able children are set at a higher level by decreasing time limits, changing distances and altering speed. In fact, able children may well find some of the activities challenging and stimulating because they are new and unfamiliar.

Thirdly, activities may be modified to accommodate a particular child's abilities. For example, a child could use a short-handled racket to hit a softball rather than a tennis racket to hit a tennis ball, or a child may work from a wheelchair while others are working from the floor.

Adaptation for particular needs

This section provides some general ideas on modifications and alterations which may be incorporated into certain lessons, according to the needs of particular children. You will note that descriptive terms – rather than the 'diagnostic conditions' – are used to categorise the suggestions. For example, 'mobility restricted' is used in preference to 'cerebral palsy'.

This is to encourage inclusion that focuses on the child's area of need, rather than on the characteristics of a medical condition (Addy and Dixon, 1999). However, as some of the terms used may be unfamiliar to some, the explanation includes the conditions where these characteristics are typically, although not always, seen.

In addition to the general suggestions below, some lesson plans offer ideas on how to adapt the particular activity in that lesson.

Mobility impaired

This group comprises children who need to use either a manual or an electric wheelchair as their main source of mobility around school. These children may be able to crawl a little, but they have a limited range of upper- and lower-limb movement when out of their chairs. This includes children with certain forms of cerebral palsy such as spastic diplegia, spastic quadriplegia, dystonia and choreo-athetoid; types of muscular dystrophy (particularly Duchennes); spina bifida; and some who have suffered a head injury. The following measures will enable these children to participate in the PE class.

◎ Encourage the child to change position as much as possible by coming out of the wheelchair onto the floor or by sitting on a stool with their learning support assistant (LSA) (if allocated) holding their hips (not trunk), allowing free movement of the upper limbs.

◎ During the warm-up, the LSA can facilitate stretching by gently encouraging the straightening of limbs, working from a position near to the body (proximal) rather than pulling hands and feet (distal).

◎ When warm-ups involve variations in speed and plane, allow the child to attempt these from the floor or to manoeuvre around using their wheelchair.

◎ Discourage W-sitting as much as possible. This is a position where the child sits on the floor, between their knees. It is discouraged because it increases the tension in the muscles surrounding the hips, can encourage hip displacement and can ultimately lead to reduced mobility. The majority of children with cerebral palsy have muscle tightness; W-sitting will aggravate this. This position also places the hamstrings, hip adductors, internal rotators and heel cords in an extremely shortened range, increasing tightness or contractures. Encourage another pattern of sitting wherever possible.

◎ Sit on the floor in supported sitting – either straight-legged with support at the hips or cross-legged (not symmetrical) – for as many activities as possible. The child may then focus on movement around the trunk and upper limbs. Certain activities can be played in a sitting position with all the class participating in the same position, for example Floor football (lesson 2) and Beach ball volleyball (lesson 9).

◎ When activities require movement around or between obstacles, the child can use the wheelchair to manoeuvre around objects; the effort and control required equates to the movements of those who do not use a wheelchair.

- Children should work with supported standing whenever possible, as many activities will enhance upper limb and trunk control while encouraging stabilisation at the hips.

- Slow-moving projectiles such as shuttlecocks, beanbags, balloons and fling socks can be used during throw-and-catch activities to accommodate motor planning and organisation.

- Activities such as the Scoop lacrosse game can be played sitting in a manual wheelchair with sides removed to allow freedom of movement. An assistant can help the child to move.

- Games such as hockey, cricket and football require a stooped physical push action and lower-limb control which may be too difficult for some children. Allow the child to use their electric or manual chair, but place a stiff sheet of card in front of the footplates to act as a buffer or kickplate. The child can then concentrate on wheelchair control while continuing to play the game.

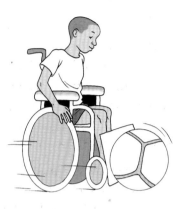

- Encourage smooth rather than jerky movements to increase the muscle tone of children with cerebral palsy. This is particularly important during the static and dynamic resistance activities such as tug o' war games.

- Attempt as many games as possible from the floor position. If these require rapid movements, reduce the number of people participating at one time in order to reduce potential collisions.

- To play games such as Colour blind, colour conscious provide a Helping Hand Reacher. These are available from Nottingham Rehab Supplies, chemist shops or occupational therapy departments, and are handy gadgets for any child who has to use a wheelchair to have on any occasion.

- When extended-arm activities are required, use arm gaiters to support arms in a straight position. These are available from occupational therapy or physiotherapy departments.

- When working on the floor in prone position (tummy down), provide a small cushion to go under the chin, or work from a mat to prevent bumps and bruises.

- Adapt games so that the child can be fully included, asking class members to contribute ideas. For example, during the On board the royal yacht game, adapted movements could include:
  - scrub the deck – reach to toes and demonstrate scrubbing action;
  - climb the mast – stretch arms above head;
  - sailor overboard – lift one arm and extend leg on same side;
  - royal visit – touch toes.

- Assistance should be provided for rolling, but physical support should focus on hips and shoulders. Use a soft mat.

- Monitor the child's energy and stamina levels carefully so that they do not become exhausted.

Mobility restricted

This group comprises children who are dependent on walking aids to extend their mobility. These walking aids include rollators, Kaye Walkers, tripods, sticks, forearm crutches, gait trainers and sit-on walkers. Many of the children who require these devices have cerebral palsy, but the group also includes those with a limb amputation, Perthes disease, early muscular dystrophy (spinal muscular atrophy or Duchennes) or arthrogryposis. These children will have some mobility, but it is restricted. They should be encouraged to use their mobility as much as possible or to work from the floor. However, care must be taken to monitor levels of fatigue, which will vary from child to child. It is important to note that where mobility requires a great deal of effort, the child will tire easily, and this needs to be appreciated in the context of the daily timetable. The following measures are recommended.

◎ Discourage W-sitting as much as possible (see above) as it will aggravate the problem of increased muscle tone.

◎ When working with children who need help to change position, ensure that you lift appropriately. Seek advice from the child's physiotherapist or occupational therapist about the correct moving and handling procedures. It is vital that the child is never lifted or lowered by being held under the arms; this changes the child's muscle tightness and can increase movement problems.

◎ Support the child in standing by holding at the hips whenever possible.

◎ In ball games, concentrate on releasing objects rather than catching them.

◎ When activities need extended arms, use arm gaiters to support the position.

◎ During wheelbarrow activities, allow the child to bear weight through elbows rather than hands.

◎ Provide a physical support such as a high-backed chair or handhold to help the child to balance on one leg.

◎ Concentrate on static one-legged balance rather than hopping.

◎ Involve the child in the cool-down activity, and encourage sitting balance by having someone sit behind the child to support their back and hips.

Some principles and strategies from the mobility-impaired category may also be relevant for some individuals.

Unilateral coordination

Some children who have cerebral palsy or who have suffered a head injury or stroke may have weakness or restricted movement down one side of their body. This is known as a hemiplegia (paralysis of the arm, leg and trunk down one side of the body) or hemiparesis (weakness down one side of the body). This asymmetrical condition may result in poor gait and difficulties with balance, as well as concerns about using both hands together (bimanual integration). A one-handed approach may be used by children who have Erbs palsy, a condition resulting from damage to the brachial plexus at birth, leaving restricted or no movement in the affected arm. This too will have implications for bilateral activities.

For this group, activities will need to be adapted to accommodate the child's specific needs. Consider the following strategies:

◎ Wherever possible, encourage symmetrical and bilateral arm movements.

◎ For as many activities as possible and appropriate, encourage children to intertwine their fingers so that their hands are positioned centrally.

- During running activities, encourage the child to grasp a rubber quoit with both hands to reduce increased tone in the affected arm.

- Use an arm gaiter to extend the affected arm during games where crawling or four-point balance is required.

- Encourage partners to sit next to the child's affected side to reinforce the child's awareness of this side of their body, thus reducing neglect and asymmetry.

- Discourage W-sitting; encourage long-legged or cross-legged sitting.

Perceptual–motor difficulties

Perceptual and motor problems are a common characteristic of children with a developmental coordination disorder (DCD). (The term **dyspraxia** may be a more familiar term – this is a type of DCD.) These children are characterised by erratic motor organisation, poor fine and gross motor coordination, and difficulties with perceptual processing (Addy, 2003). Despite these difficulties, children with DCD usually have average or above average intelligence, and are therefore acutely aware that their skills are not as well developed as those of their peers. Perceptual and motor difficulties can also be seen in children with Williams syndrome, cerebral palsy (particularly children with left-sided hemiplegia or hemiparesis) and autism, and may be seen in children with dyslexia.

Difficulties in perceptual–motor functioning will affect hand–eye coordination, foot–eye coordination, form constancy, visual and auditory figure–ground discrimination, body imagery, and judgement of space. This must be taken into account during the PE lesson, and the following strategies are recommended:

- Provide the child with a base station or carpet square to provide a safe base from which to work.

- Children with visual–spatial difficulties will find listening and moving simultaneously quite difficult. They should therefore be positioned near to the teacher so that both verbal and non-verbal prompts can be provided to reinforce an action.

- Activities such as Flap-a-fish and Fish o' war that involve forward leaning may prove uncomfortable because of the child's spatial difficulties. Provide support so that the child does not overbalance and topple forward.

- Children with perceptual–motor difficulties may need longer to process information and may feel unable to respond quickly enough in games such as Pigs can fly?, Countdown and Find it, owing to their inability to discriminate objects rapidly. If this is a particular concern, omit the competitive element, encouraging children to achieve all actions successfully.

- Weight bearing through extended arms is required in activities such as wheelbarrows, and this will be particularly problematic for children with low muscle tone or shoulder-girdle instability. Allow an adult or taller child to work with the child, holding the thighs or hips (rather than ankles) to offer increased support. Reduce the distance to be travelled if movement is demanded.

- Difficulties with body image or schema may make it hard for a child to move their body into certain positions because they are unsure of where their limbs are in space. Physical guidance may be needed, for example during the Letter shapes game. To help reinforce body schema further, take digital photos of movement positions and show them to the child immediately. (These do not have to be retained.) Alternatively, video the session and then watch it together with the child, discussing how they can adjust positioning and thus further motor control.

- Some children with spatial organisation difficulties may find the whole class moving simultaneously somewhat overwhelming. If this seems apparent, put the class into two groups so that fewer pupils are moving at one time.

- Some children may struggle to respond as quickly as others to non-verbal commands, as in the Traffic lights game. Allow these children a short 'running on' concession.

- Balancing a beanbag on the head during games such as Frozen beanbag will require more effort for those with coordination difficulties. Emphasise controlled movement rather than speedy reactions.

- Children with memory difficulties may struggle to recall sequences of actions and therefore will need a physical demonstration to aid memory. Ask the child to demonstrate with you what is expected to the rest of the class. This multisensory emphasis will aid recall.

Children with spatial difficulties will need support to walk along a low gym bench and further guidance to step over or around any obstacles on the gym bench. It is therefore important that adult support or an empathetic peer is available to walk alongside, offering a hand to hold if required. Children with poor motor coordination may struggle to produce the correct movements to meander in and out of obstacles in games such as Thread the buckle. Provide an additional physical and/or verbal prompt to help the child accomplish this task; for example: 'Thread this leg [touch the left leg] through the hoop first. Step in with this leg [touch the right leg].'

Sensory modulation

There may be children in your classroom who seem to have unusual needs that affect their participation in PE, but whose exact difficulty is hard to pinpoint. These are often children who have problems with interpreting sensations, particularly touch, and who may therefore respond in quite extreme ways. Sensory modulation is the name given to our body's ability to integrate the information we receive through touch, taste, vision, hearing and smell. Many children with DCD, ADHD, fragile-X syndrome, Williams syndrome, Down syndrome or an autistic spectrum disorder (ASD) experience difficulties with this, and they usually present in one of three ways:

- **Tactile defensiveness** – children who are tactile defensive avoid certain textures such as those that are scratchy and rough. They are acutely sensitive to touch and such contact can almost hurt. These children avoid contact with others, evade anticipated touch and keep away from occupations which may involve body contact, preferring solitary play (Royeen and Lane, 1991).

- **Sensory defensiveness** – in contrast to children who have a very specific reaction to touch, there are others who are oversensitive (hypersensitive) to any sensory stimulation such as sounds, sights and smells (tastes will also be affected). These children may hate loud noises, sudden clapping, cheers and surprise bangs; likewise strong odours or any overstimulating environment may induce a reaction. The PE class characterises such a situation.

- **Sensory dormancy** – some children have the opposite problem in that they are undersensitive to sensory stimulation (hyposensitive) and in order to gain some feedback from touch and sound, they will crash around, bumping into things. These are the children you often hear coming before you see them, who are ham fisted and heavy footed.

To help children with sensory modulation disorders, employ the following strategies:

- Children with poor sensory modulation will need to stimulate their muscles prior to any action. Encourage children to rub their arms, trunk and legs vigorously but briefly between activities; this will enhance their body awareness and improve accuracy of positioning.
- Incorporate and encourage slow, rhythmic movements (rather than fast, jerky ones) into warm-up activities and in resistance games such as Tug o' war and Sumo circle.
- Any activities incorporating touch should incorporate deep pressure rather than light touch.
- Joint traction and compression – for example, the sort of pressure exerted through the shoulders when attempting a wheelbarrow – and vigorous rubbing will all help with sensory modulation (Stagnitti et al., 1999).
- Children experiencing kinaesthetic regulation problems will have difficulty knowing how much effort to exert when throwing, so their aim and direction may appear erratic. Grade these activities using different projectiles such as beanbags, balloons, fling socks and heavyweight foam balls. Heavier projectiles will afford more control. Initially encourage accurate underarm throwing techniques, providing physical demonstration.
- When developing ball skills, place these children at the periphery of the group. If their ball goes astray, it will be less likely to disturb the others, thus reducing the possibility of the child's being teased.
- Slow down the pace of the hand–feet placement during the Bunny hop activity, so that the child has time to organise movements. Provide verbal prompts, for example 'Hands, feet, hands, feet' – according to the movement required in the sequence.

In addition, employ the following strategies for children who are tactile defensive:

- All activities require some form of touch, so be aware that children who have tactile sensitivity may find this stressful. Where possible, try to warn the child before they are touched, in order to prepare for the reaction. The touch should always be firm; light touch can be experienced as painful by children with heightened tactile sensation.
- In the Body words activity, allow the tactile-defensive child to be positioned either at the beginning or end of the word so that they are likely to be touched only on one side, rather than being pressed between two 'letters'.
- Be careful to observe the children who are tactile defensive to check whether they are comfortable with the contact involved in the games. If the class becomes very excited, they are likely to grab and squeeze other children in their group – which may distress the tactile-defensive child.
- Beware of jostling, which will distress children who are tactile defensive. If this is an issue, restrict the number of children moving at one time.

Attention and concentration difficulties

There seems to be an increasing number of children who struggle with attention and concentration in school, a trend highlighted by the rise in the number of those diagnosed with ADHD. Children with ADHD struggle to maintain their attention and are easily distracted by irrelevant auditory information. This, together with their poor visual attention, causes some concern in PE lessons. The issue for children with ADHD is not necessarily one of over activity (Harvey and Reid, 2003); rather, they are unable to focus long enough to absorb the instructions for the activity in which they are asked to participate. In addition to poor short-term memory – which affects the child's capacity to learn routines and skills – the overwhelming auditory and visual stimuli in a typical PE class can easily result in such a child becoming overloaded, excitable and quite possibly disruptive. These children need a teaching combination which incorporates sensory–motor control and gross-motor-skills training (Korkman and Pesonen, 1994). There are several modifications and adaptations that will help in a class setting:

- Use a base station or carpet square to encourage the child to maintain a position between activities.

- Children with ADHD may have poor observation skills and so may need a more directive partner to help them obtain certain postures and movements.

- Provide a verbal warning (or prompt) before any potentially noisy activity which may overexcite the child.

- Limit the number of children who move at any one time, thus reducing the amount of visual and auditory stimulation.

- If a series of instructions is given, ask children to repeat it back to ensure the instructions have been understood and retained.

- Provide support in the form of an adult or appropriate peer who will help by providing prompts and reminders of the task in hand throughout each lesson.

- Children with ADHD may become particularly 'giddy' during exciting, competitive games. Restrict the number of children who play at one time, and give the child a specific role – such as scorekeeper, judge or buddy – which will occupy them while they wait for their turn.

- Children with ADHD may get overexuberant when throwing or transferring an object: emphasise controlled projection rather than speed.

- Encourage controlled passing using a small sand bag rather than a beanbag. The added weight should require more effort for projection.

- Include as many kinaesthetic activities as possible. Increased pressure through the limbs has a calming effect and aids motor control. Resistance work is particularly useful, although care must be taken to ensure that movements are smooth and not jerky.

- Limit the area of work so that the child is confined to working within a restricted area where energy is spent on control rather than 'filling the space'.

- During ball-based activities, place the child on the periphery of the group so they are less likely to be distracted by flying projectiles.

- Give the child an active position during competitive games. In Crocker, for example, the backstop is usually a demanding position.

- In activities such as Throw and flick, children with ADHD may flick objects such as nets and towels erratically due to poor proprioception and fleeting attention. Provide the child with a larger towel (e.g. a bath sheet) or net which will require more effort than a small towel. The increased effort should increase control.

- Attention and control will be harnessed by the suitable selection of an able partner during activities such as Foosball and Three-legged football.

- Provide a physical prompt, such as a tap on the child's left or right shoulder, to indicate direction of actions in games such as Beat the bunny and On board the royal yacht.

- Slow down movements to improve control. Emphasise control rather than speed, perhaps adding forfeits for sloppy control.

- In foot- or hand-placement activities, provide the child with an outline of a foot drawn on stiff card and encourage them to cut it out while they are waiting for their turn. The effort of cutting a material stiffer than paper will demand more muscular effort and aid fine motor control.

- Use digital photography and/or video to give feedback to guide and adjust motor control.

- During activities which require sequential memory, encourage rehearsal of actions. The child can either quietly chant the movements to be remembered or act them out with the child who is 'on', for example during Chinese whispers, and I went to market.

- Continuous engagement with the task will prevent the child losing concentration and going off track.

- Encourage the child to help set out and clear away the equipment used in the lesson. The heavy weights involved will stimulate proprioception and have a calming, controlling effect.

Comprehension

Many children who attend mainstream schools have either subtle or very recognisable communication and/or comprehension difficulties. Careful use of language in the lessons is therefore vital. Children who have Asperger syndrome, semantic–pragmatic language disorder or one of the other autistic spectrum disorders will interpret instructions literally. Requests such as 'Can you form a circle?' may elicit the response 'Yes' – *without* the action. It is important to gain specific advice from the child's speech and language therapist in order to communicate effectively and appreciate the particular nuances of the child's comprehension. The following measures will help:

- Keep instructions simple, clear and consistent. They may be supported by physical demonstration or a non-verbal prompt, such as a gesture, sign or touch.

- Ensure that children have an understanding of movement concepts, and add to the repertoire only when the child has fully understood their meaning.

- Remember that for children who interpret language literally, some games – for example, Wink murder – will seem very confusing.

- Imagination may be limited to the child's actual life experiences, so activities which involve pretence may prove problematic. In this situation, use events familiar to the child.

- Partner the child with an empathetic buddy who will help guide their movements.

- Do not force the child into participating if they appear uncomfortable or unsure about its purpose.

- Encourage teams to be careful in including any child who may have limited comprehension, rather than forcing them into a position or action against their will.

For children in all the areas mentioned, further guidance should be sought from a specialist teacher, local paediatric occupational therapist, physiotherapist, or speech and language therapist regarding specific concerns.

Assessing progress

The motor skills checklist on page 35 presents a series of basic motor tasks which most children should be able to achieve by the end of Key Stage 1 (Year 2; age 7 years). The checklist may be used in several ways.

By using the checklist to observe and record each child's motor abilities at the beginning of each school term, you will be able to identify specific areas of motor coordination to work on in the following term's scheme of work.

The checklist may be used as an outcome measure when the *Get Physical!* programme is used in its entirety, within either a school context or a therapeutic setting. In this case, the number of tasks which the child is able to achieve can be compared at the beginning and end of the programme.

The checklist will help in identifying those children with apparent difficulties in motor coordination, for whom advice and guidance from a paediatric occupational therapist or physiotherapist should be sought.

Parents and carers could use the checklist to evaluate their own child's physical abilities. It may be possible to request that they assess their child's motor competence before commencing Reception and again before Years 1 and 2. Their assessments will provide a baseline from which to start in the PE lessons. Parents and carers can then be active in setting goals and tasks for their child. Engaging parents and carers in assessing and developing their child's physical abilities as well as their intellectual ones can have very positive outcomes.

Teachers who work with children with specific motor coordination difficulties such as DCD may find the checklist helpful as a rough guide to motor aptitude, but a more detailed analysis of motor abilities may be required. Standardised measures, such as the Movement Assessment Battery for Children (M-ABC) (Henderson and Sugden, 1992), may be used in collaboration with the child's occupational therapist or physiotherapist to identify particular areas of ability and difficulty.

For children who have motor difficulties with a neurological basis, such as those with cerebral palsy, the checklist may be used as a guide to 'normal' movement. These children may also require a more detailed analysis of motor skills using more refined standardised measures such as the Gross Motor Function Measure (Russell *et al.*, 2002). This assessment can be undertaken by the child's occupational therapist or physiotherapist.

Children with degenerative conditions such as muscular dystrophy (Duchennes) need to focus on maintaining as well as progressing physical capabilities. The aim of accomplishing all tasks on the list may be unrealistic, owing to the nature of the condition; this should not deter the child from trying to reach the goals identified.

Motor skills checklist

Name .... Year ....

Age on assessment .... Date of assessment ....

Observations made by ....

Key skill The child can:	Able	Unable
run around the room and stop on command		
run around the room without collision		
alter speed of movement on command		
manoeuvre around objects without collision		
alter plane of movement on command, i.e. high, low		
appreciate spatial concepts such as up, down, beside		
skip (not using a rope) around the room		
throw a beanbag to a target 3m away		
catch a beanbag thrown from 3m away		
throw a football to a target 3m away		
catch a football thrown from 3m away		
throw a small ball to a target 3m away		
catch a small ball thrown from 3m away		
bounce a ball and catch it		
hit a moving ball with a short-handled bat		
hit a moving ball with a long-handled bat		
jump forwards with feet together (3 jumps)		
jump backwards (3 jumps)		
kick a football into a goal from 3m away		
intercept and stop a moving football using one foot		
strike a moving football in an specified direction		
dribble a football with control (alternating feet)		
balance on the right leg for 15 seconds		
balance on the left leg for 15 seconds		
hop forwards (3 hops)		
alternately hop and jump (hopscotch)		
walk along a 5m line with heel–toe gait		

Key skill The child can:	Able	Unable
maintain balance on all 4 limbs and raise the right leg, holding for 15 seconds		
maintain balance on all 4 limbs and raise the left leg, holding for 15 seconds		
maintain balance on all 4 limbs and raise the right arm, holding for 15 seconds		
maintain balance on all 4 limbs and raise the left arm, holding for 15 seconds		
maintain a wheelbarrow position for 5 seconds		
walk unsupported (safely) along a low gym bench		
demonstrate a sense of rhythm		
roll sideways		
perform a forward roll		
follow a simple sequence of 3 actions		
create a simple sequence of movements		
appreciate rules of simple team games		
take turns		

Additional notes:

3 Lesson plans

Observation and listening skills

Area: *Games*

Objectives:

✳ to develop concentration and listening skills, stressing their importance when developing movement skills;

✳ to develop group cooperation;

✳ to encourage observation and attention.

Equipment:

✳ penny whistle, or recorder or other wind instrument.

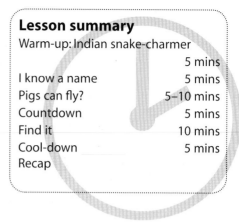

Lesson summary

Warm-up: Indian snake-charmer
                                    5 mins
I know a name   5 mins
Pigs can fly?   5–10 mins
Countdown   5 mins
Find it   10 mins
Cool-down   5 mins
Recap

Activity	Purpose	Curriculum links: *England* / Scotland
Warm-up: Indian snake-charmer ◎ All children curl up on the floor, making themselves as small as possible. ◎ Using a penny whistle (or recorder or other wind instrument), pretend to be an Indian snake-charmer. Children slowly extend from their curled position to an upright stretched posture, moving to the music. ◎ Whenever the music stops, the children must recoil slowly. Vary the volume of the music to encourage children to listen well.	Warming up the muscles through guided stretch activities which require concentration and attention to the music *1a, 1b, 2a, 2b, 6b* *1a, 3a*	
I know a name ◎ The children sit in a circle on the floor. ◎ One child starts a clapping rhythm and chants: 'I know a name'. The class repeat: 'I know a name'. The lead child concludes: 'I know a name and it sounds like this …' and claps out the syllables of their name; e.g. Steph-a-nie (3 claps). ◎ The next child in the circle then takes the lead. Clapping should be continuous, with one child quickly following another. ◎ At the end of the cycle, the children can take turns to clap out the name of someone in the group whilst everyone else guesses whose name it is.	Developing a sense of rhythm and encouraging listening skills *2a, 2b, 6b* *3b, 4a, 5b*	

Activity	Purpose	Curriculum links:
		England / Scotland
Pigs can fly? This game is a modified version of Simon says, in which children decide whether an animal or object can or cannot fly. ◎ Call out a series of animals and objects, stating that each one can fly; e.g. 'Planes fly', 'Spiders fly'. After each, the children decide whether or not it can really fly – and show their decision by either flapping their arms or keeping them down; e.g. 'Ducks fly' (all children should be flapping arms), 'Seagulls fly' (continue to flap), 'Pigs fly' (children who continue to flap are out). ◎ Children who are caught flapping when they should be still sit out.	Developing listening skills and the ability to process information while performing an action	*2b, 2c* 3a, 4b
Countdown ◎ Explain to the children that they have until you count to 5 to find and touch something in the room. You will tell them what sort of thing to touch each time. ◎ Call out an adjective, then count down: '5, 4, 3, 2, 1, beep, beep, beep, time up!' You could ask children to find and touch items that are, e.g., red, large, cold, wet, triangular, fluffy, or flat.	Developing listening skills, observation skills, organisation and motor planning	*2b, 2c, 7a* 2b, 3a
Find it ◎ Children sit on the floor around the edge of the room in teams of 4. You stand in the middle. ◎ Call out an object for the teams to find. The first team to send a team member to you with that object get a point. You could ask for an obvious object such as a cone, football or hoop, or a more obscure object such as a tied shoelace or a fair hair and a dark hair. ◎ The team with the most points are the winners.	Developing listening skills, group cooperation, speed and anticipation	*2a, 2b, 2c, 7a* 4b, 5a
Cool-down ◎ Children find a space and lie on their backs on the floor with eyes closed. ◎ Encourage them to listen to the noises in the room. ◎ Comment on sounds in the environment, starting with distant sounds and gradually leading to near ones, such as breathing.	Developing relaxation and listening skills	*4b* 6a

Recap   *3a, 3b, 3c, 4a, 4b*   6a

- Discuss the importance of listening carefully in order to succeed. Talk about how it can be difficult to listen when there is a lot of noise or activity going on – you have to concentrate extra hard. Ask the children if they can think of a time when they experienced this. (Take note of children who express concerns regarding listening in classroom, as this can be partially rectified by strategic seating arrangements.)

- Discuss the sounds children hear when they wake up in the morning. Can they remember what they are?

- You might suggest making a sound-match game. Children fill either yoghurt cartons or covered jars with different items, then ask others to guess the contents of each by listening to the sound when the carton or jar is shaken.

Lesson 2

Ball propulsion (push)

Objectives:

❋ to develop hip-girdle stability and flexibility;

❋ to control low-level ball propulsion;

❋ to increase shoulder strength and control.

Equipment:

❋ cones to act as goalposts;

❋ marking tape or chalk;

❋ large foam balls – 1 each for half of the class.

Lesson summary

Warm-up: Putty	5 mins
Roll and shift	5–10 mins
Rolie goalie	5–10 mins
Floor football	10–15 mins
Cool-down	5 mins
Recap	

Activity	Purpose	Curriculum links: England / Scotland
Warm-up: Putty ◎ Say to the children, 'Imagine you are a ball of stretchy putty and you are about to be pulled in all sorts of directions. Start by lying on the floor on your back. Now curl up tightly into a ball, with your knees tucked under your chin. Slowly stretch out one arm … then the other. Stretch out one leg … then the other. Imagine you are being really stretched. When I clap, you will quickly spring back into a ball shape so you are curled up tightly again.' ◎ Instruct the children to stretch and spring back 3 times. ◎ Try it again the other way up, with faces to the floor.	Warming up and stretching limbs	*1a, 1b, 2b, 2c* *1a, 1b*
Roll and shift ◎ Children sit on the floor with legs apart, each with a partner sitting opposite in the same position. They roll a large foam ball to each other 3 times, then move back 0.25m. ◎ Repeat several times, increasing the distance each time. Also try using alternate hands to roll the ball. Point out that the further apart they are, the more effort is required to roll and target the ball.	Strengthening abdominal muscles and hips while increasing strength of shoulder girdle	*1a, 1b, 2b, 7a* *1a, 2a, 3a, 4a*
Rolie goalie ◎ Set up a series of goals (the number will depend on the number of teams) using cones positioned approximately 2m apart. Using marking tape or chalk, draw several lines opposite and parallel to the goal at the following distances: 2m, 3m, 4m and 5m.	Encouraging propulsion and accurate targeting skills with alternate hands	

Activity	Purpose	Curriculum links: *England / Scotland*
◎ Put the class into teams of 4–6 children and give each team a large foam ball. ◎ Each child takes it in turn to sit on the line closest to the goal. They then must attempt to push the ball along the floor into the goal using their right hand. If successful, their team receives 1 point. The ball is retrieved and passed on to the next child, who shuffles forward to the line for their turn. ◎ Once all the team members have attempted to score a goal with their right hand, they all try again with their left hand. ◎ When all children have attempted to score a goal with each hand, they repeat the process, from the 3m marker, then from the 4m and 5m markers. ◎ The team with the most points win the game.		*1b, 2a, 2b, 7a, 7c* *2a, 2b, 3a, 3b, 5a*

Floor football

◎ Create a small football pitch (approx 9m x 9m) with marking tape or chalk. Draw a central line dividing the halves and place a goal at each end.

◎ Put the class into small teams of approximately 7 children. Each team should have 3 defenders, 3 attackers and 1 goalkeeper. After choosing their positions, the children sit on the floor in the appropriate places. Once positioned, they must not move. (Ideally they should sit cross-legged.)

◎ The game is played by pushing a foam ball from one end of the pitch to the other to score a goal, using the arms only. The ball must be kept at a low level at all times and must not be kicked. As this is quite tiring, change teams once a goal has been scored.

This game requires considerable trunk control to allow for stretch in varying directions.

It is very important that they keep their bottoms in the same position on the floor throughout the game.

A lot of effort and control is required in the upper limbs.

1a, 1b, 2a, 2b, 7a, 7b, 7c
1a, 2a, 2b, 3a, 3b, 5a

Activity	Purpose	Curriculum links: *England* / Scotland
Cool-down ◎ Children find a space on the floor and lie on their backs with arms at their sides and eyes closed. ◎ Give instructons as follows: 'Stretch your right arm down as far as you can, hold and count to 5. Do the same with your left arm … now your right leg … your left leg … now with both arms … and with both legs. Relax and take 5 deep breaths. Stand up and shake all your limbs.'	Calming activity	*1a, 1b* 1b, 2a

Recap   *3a, 3b, 3c, 4a, 4b*   1b, 6a

- Ask the children which parts of their body were doing the most work during the lesson.

- Ask why they think it is important to strengthen control in their upper limbs. Refer to aspects of gymnastics such as handstands, forward rolls and bridges; targeting when throwing a ball; and activities requiring fine motor skills, such as handwriting, art work, practical maths and science.

- Ask if it was it hard to get the ball past the opposition in Floor football. What was the best way to achieve this? Discuss strategy rather than strength.

Lesson 3

Accurate throw 1

Objectives:

✳ to develop hand–eye coordination;

✳ to develop propulsion skills;

✳ to assess spatial relationships.

Equipment:

✳ beanbags – 1 for each child (ideally use only 2 colours);

✳ 8–10 coloured hula hoops, or coloured mats (e.g. Spordas Space Stations™);

✳ marking tape or chalk;

✳ 2 chairs;

✳ 3 skittles, or empty washing-up-liquid bottles.

Lesson summary

Warm-up: Knees up	5 mins
Throw and catch	5 mins
Hoopla	5 mins
Tic, tac, toe	10 mins
Beanbag skittles	10 mins
Cool-down	5 mins
Recap	

Activity	Purpose	Curriculum links: *England* / Scotland
Warm-up: Knees up ◉ Children walk on the spot, bringing their knees up as high as possible. They tap the right knee with the right hand, and the left knee with the left hand. ◉ Repeat, tapping each knee with the opposite hand. Then increase speed so that the children are running on the spot. ◉ Finish with 5 star jumps, clapping the hands together when feet are jumped together.	Warming up the muscles to prepare for action Developing the ability to transfer the right hand across the body to touch the limbs on the left side, and vice versa (midline crossing) Bringing hands to the middle of the trunk (the midline) in preparation to catch an object	*1a, 1b, 2a* 1a, 2a, 3a
Throw and catch ◉ In pairs, the children try to pass a beanbag to each other without dropping it, starting approximately 0.5m apart. ◉ After 3 successful catches, each pair takes a small step back to increase the distance slightly. They continue until they are 5m apart.	By using a beanbag rather than a ball, introducing aspects of weight and tactile quality into throwing and catching	*1a, 1b, 2b, 7a* 2a, 3a, 5a
Hoopla ◉ Scatter coloured hula hoops around the room, and give each child a beanbag. ◉ Ask the children to find a place to stand (outside the hoops) and then to stay there. ◉ When you call out a colour, the children try to throw their beanbag into the nearest hoop of that colour. They continue to throw until successful, then all retrieve their bags, ready to hear the next colour called. ◉ Alternatively, coloured mats may be used as target areas. You can then call out a colour or a shape.	Developing targeting skills within a relatively wide area	*1a, 1b, 2b, 7a* 2a, 3a, 3b, 5a

Activity	Purpose	Curriculum links: *England / Scotland*
Tic, tac, toe	Developing accurate targeting skills and turn taking	
◎ Using marking tape or chalk, create several noughts and crosses grids on floor. For each grid, draw a playing line 1m away.	Enhancing hand–eye coordination	
◎ Divide the class into small teams of 3 or 4.		
◎ Put 2 teams on each grid and give a set of beanbags of one colour to the 'noughts' and a set of another colour to the 'crosses'.		
◎ Teams take turns to throw a bag into a square, with team members taking turns in rotation. The first team to get 3 of their beanbags in a row, vertically, horizontally or diagonally, are the winners.	*1a, 1b, 2b, 2c, 7a, 7c* *2a, 2b, 3a, 3b, 5a*	
Beanbag skittles	Refining specific targeting skills from a distance and height	
◎ Put 2 chairs facing each other at opposite ends of the room, about 4m apart. Place a beanbag on each chair. Appoint a supporter to stand behind each chair. (This could be an adult helper.) Place a row of 3 skittles (or washing-up liquid bottles) halfway between the chairs.	Encouraging teamwork and cooperation	
◎ Put the class in two teams and seat each team on one side of room so they can observe the chairs and skittles. Number the children in each team so that each child has a partner in the opposing team.		
◎ When you call out a number, those two children run to the chairs allocated to their team, stand on them and throw the beanbag to try to knock over a skittle. The first to topple a skittle wins their team a point.		
◎ If the skittle is not knocked over, the child retrieves the beanbag, gets back on the chair and throws again. They do this until a skittle is toppled. The player must be standing on the chair when throwing the beanbag.		
◎ Numbers are called out at random, but every child should have a turn.		
◎ The supporter standing behind each chair should ensure that the seat, or child, does not topple as players rush to take their turn.		

1a, 1b, 2b, 2c, 7a, 7b, 7c
2a, 2b, 3a, 3b, 4b, 5a

Activity	Purpose	Curriculum links: *England* / Scotland
Cool-down ◎ Children sit on the floor with legs straight out in front. When their personal number (from the previous game) is called, they stretch up with both arms together, lean forward, count to 5 and rest. They do this 3 times. Several numbers can be called out at a time.	Stretching and relaxing the muscles of the upper legs and arms	*1a, 1b* *1b, 2a*

Recap   *3a, 3b, 3c, 4a, 4b*   *3a, 6a*

- Discuss how the lesson started with an easy task, but gradually got harder and harder, especially when it came to throwing the beanbag accurately.

- What made the throw successful? Refer to being in the right position, taking time, accurately assessing the distance, and throwing with the right amount of effort. Relate this to other games such as Frisbee and Piggy in the middle.

- Suggest that, as in many tasks, it is better to stop and think rather than rushing. Can children give any examples of when it is important to do this? (Examples might include losing your temper, rushing lunch, scribbling work.)

Additional differentiation

- If children have restricted mobility, support standing for targeting practice, and let them sit on the chair, rather than stand, to play Beanbag skittles.

- For children with sensory modulation difficulties, a heavier beanbag could be used to increase feedback through the muscles of the arm (proprioception).

- Standing on the chair to play Beanbag skittles will be particularly difficult for children with visuo–spatial difficulties, and a physical support should be provided. Alternatively, they could throw from a standing position in front of, rather than on, the chair.

Accurate throw 2

Area: *Games*

Objectives:

✻ to throw a ball at a target;

✻ to assess the speed and direction of a ball;

✻ to accommodate spatial planning and organisation.

Equipment:

✻ footballs – 1 each for half of the class;

✻ marking tape or chalk;

✻ 2 large foam balls and 2 small foam balls;

✻ 1 cricket bat;

✻ 1 tennis ball.

Lesson summary	
Warm-up: Fit fives	5 mins
Bounce and catch	5 mins
Name game	5 mins
Dodge square (a)	10 mins
Dodge square (b)	10 mins
French cricket	5 mins
Cool-down	5 mins
Recap	

Activity	**Purpose** Curriculum links: *England* / Scotland
Warm-up: Fit fives ◉ Children gently jog on the spot, gradually increasing speed. This is followed by: 　　5 jumps on the spot; 　　5 star jumps; 　　5 star jumps adding a clap as arms meet above and below; 　　5 stretches up and then down to toes. ◉ Finish with everyone running round the room, changing direction on command.	Warming up muscles, particularly those of upper limbs *1a, 1b* 1a, 2a
Bounce and catch ◉ Put the children into pairs and provide each pair with a football. ◉ Starting at a distance of 1.5m apart, the children in each pair bounce the ball to one another. ◉ Following 3 successful catches, both players take a small step backwards. They continue until they have achieved a bounce across 4–5m.	Developing effective passing skills Success is dependent upon the effective targeting of the ball. *1a, 1b, 2b, 7a* 2a, 2b, 3a, 3b, 5a
Name game ◉ All children stand in a circle; you stand in the centre. ◉ Pass a football very quickly to and from individual children, calling out the child's name with each throw. ◉ Repeat, bouncing the ball back and forth.	Increasing the speed and accuracy of ball throwing *1a, 1b, 2b, 2c, 7a, 7b* 2a, 2b, 3a, 3b, 4b, 5a

Activity	Purpose	Curriculum links: *England* / Scotland

Dodge square (a)

◎ Use either marking tape or chalk to create a square half the size of a volleyball court (approx. 9m x 9m).

◎ Have 8 children (the 'targetters') standing just outside the square. The rest of the class stand inside.

◎ The group of targetters have 1 or 2 large foam balls, which they aim at the lower legs of children in the square. Make it clear that the ball must not be thrown with force. The children in the square must try to dodge the ball; if hit below the knee, they join the targetters on the outside of the square and help with catching those left inside. The last child in the square is the winner.

Developing targeting skills and avoidance tactics

1a, 1b, 2b, 2c, 7a, 7b, 7c
2a, 2b, 3a, 3b, 4b, 5a

Dodge square (b)

◎ Play as game (a), but using small foam balls.

Developing targeting skills and avoidance tactics

1a, 1b, 2b, 2c, 7a, 7b, 7c
2a, 2b, 3a, 3b, 4b, 5a

French cricket

◎ Choose a child to stand in the middle of the room with legs together and a cricket bat to protect their lower legs. Once in position, the batter must not move their feet.

◎ The rest of the class take turns to aim a tennis ball at the area between the heel and knee of the batter, who must use the cricket bat as protection.

◎ The batter is out when they are hit between knee and ankle.

As the previous two games are fast and require considerable energy, the final game demands effective targeting skills but at a calmer pace.

1a, 1b, 2b, 2c, 7a, 7b, 7c
2a, 2b, 3a, 3b, 4b, 5a

Activity	Purpose	Curriculum links:
		England / Scotland
Cool-down ◎ Children stand in a space. They bend down to touch their toes, then slowly stretch up tall, inhaling deeply as they do so. They slowly exhale as they bend down to touch their toes again. ◎ Repeat 5 times.	Relaxing muscles and calming breathing	*1a, 1b* 1b, 2a

Recap   *3a, 3b, 3c, 4a, 4b*   6a

- Explain how increasing skill was required through the lesson as the target and the ball became smaller.

- Explain that when learning any new skill, it is important to start with small steps and gradually build on these. Use the example of learning to ride a bike. Choose a learning task familiar to the children, e.g. swimming, and together decide on the steps required to achieve it.

- Discuss how success at each stage is an achievement in itself. Ask the children to think of activities in which they are learning something but have not yet reached their final goal, e.g. reaching a particular score or level in a computer game. Use the examples to discuss how each person has different abilities, and how it is important not to be negative about the abilities of others just because they are not the same as our own. This may be taken further in Circle Time.

Additional differentiation

- Children with limited mobility can target from a seated position during Dodge square games.

- Children who have restricted upper-limb function should focus on accurate manual release rather than catch.

Catch

Area: *Games*

Objectives:

✱ to develop bilateral coordination;

✱ to extend hand–eye coordination;

✱ to expand motor planning and organisation skills.

Equipment:

✱ plastic scoops – 1 for each child (use plastic scoop sets or collect empty 1 litre or 2 litre plastic milk cartons, wash thoroughly and cut each in half to create a scoop with handle);

✱ beanbags – 1 each for half of the class;

✱ small foam balls – 1 each for half of the class;

✱ marking tape or chalk;

✱ coloured tabards or team bands;

✱ 2 adjustable target nets (e.g. Tippin Targets™) or large buckets.

Lesson summary

Warm-up: Animal actions	5 mins
Circle flick and catch	5 mins
Scoopy-do	20 mins total
Scoop lacrosse	10 mins
Cool-down	5 mins
Recap	

Activity	Purpose	Curriculum links: *England* / Scotland
Warm-up: Animal actions ◉ Children move around the room: 　galloping like a horse; 　jumping like a kangaroo; 　hopping like a rabbit; 　sidestepping like a crab; 　leaping like a frog.	Warming up muscles through movement in different planes and directions and at different speeds	*1a, 1b, 2b* 1a, 1b, 2a
Circle flick and catch ◉ The children stand in a circle; you stand in the centre with a scoop. ◉ Each child takes it in turn to throw a beanbag to you. You catch it in the scoop, then throw it back to the next child. ◉ Ensure each child gets the opportunity to throw and catch the beanbag.	Demonstrating the motion required to throw and catch the beanbag using the scoop	*1a, 1b, 2b, 2c, 7a* 2a, 3a, 3b
Scoopy-do (a) – beanbag and hands ◉ The children get into pairs. One child holds the scoop and the other a beanbag. ◉ Standing 1m apart, they practise throwing the beanbag and catching it with the scoop. After 3 successive successful catches, each child takes a small step back, thus increasing the challenge. ◉ Continue to a distance of 4m.	Developing the ability to project an object and to moderate the pressure required to enable someone else to catch the object	*1a, 1b, 2b, 2c, 7a, 7b* 2a, 2b, 3a, 3b, 4b, 5a

Activity	Purpose	Curriculum links: England / Scotland
Scoopy-do (b) – beanbag and scoop ◎ Continuing in pairs (although these may be changed), both children have a scoop and must flick and catch the beanbag using the scoops. Again, they take a step back after 3 successful catches. ◎ Continue to a distance of 4m.	Developing ability to project an object and to moderate the pressure required to enable someone else to catch the object	*1a, 1b, 2b, 2c, 7a, 7b* *2a, 2b, 3a, 3b, 4b, 5a*
Scoopy-do (c) – ball and hands ◎ As Scoopy-do (a), but using a small foam ball rather than a beanbag.	Developing adaptation of movements to accommodate a more mobile, less reliable object	*1a, 1b, 2b, 2c, 7a, 7b* *2a, 2b, 3a, 3b, 4b, 5a*
Scoopy-do (d) – ball and scoop ◎ As Scoopy-do (b), but using a small foam ball rather than a beanbag.	Developing adaptation of movements to accommodate a more mobile, less reliable object	*1a, 1b, 2b, 2c, 7a, 7b* *2a, 2b, 3a, 3b, 4b, 5a*
Scoop lacrosse ◎ Using marking tape or chalk, mark out a small court 6m x 12m, and then divide it in half. ◎ Put the class into teams of about 8. Give each child a scoop. Identify each team using coloured tabards or bands. ◎ Place a target net (or bucket) at each end. Either a small soft ball or a beanbag can be used for this activity, depending upon the children's abilities. ◎ Each team must try to score a goal by passing the beanbag or ball to their team members using their scoops until one person throws it into the target net. ◎ When a player has received the beanbag or ball, they may take 2 steps only before passing to another player. Any more than 2 steps is classed as a foul, and a free throw is allocated to the opposing team. ◎ Change teams once a goal has been scored.	Developing coordination and motor planning, and team cooperation Encouraging attacking and defending *1a, 1b, 2b, 2c, 7a, 7b, 7c* *1a, 2a, 2b, 3a, 3b, 5a, 5b*

Activity	Purpose	Curriculum links: *England* / Scotland

Cool-down

◎ Children find a space and lie face down on the floor.

◎ Ask them to raise their arms, legs and neck slowly upwards, hold for 5 seconds and then relax. Repeat 5 times.

◎ They roll onto their backs. Again, ask them to raise arms, legs and neck, hold for 5 seconds and then relax.

Extending and relaxing muscles in both prone (lying face down) and supine (lying face up) positions

1a, 1b, 2b
1b, 2a

Recap   *3a, 3b, 3c, 4a, 4b*   3a, 6a

- Discuss whether it was easier to catch a beanbag or a soft ball. Why were there differences?

- Encourage children to practise throwing and catching in the playground and at home. They could use a scoop and beanbag, or a home-made scoop and a rolled-up pair of socks.

Additional differentiation

- Children who have significant problems with hand–eye coordination may struggle to catch any projectile, whether a ball or a beanbag. Focus on catching, using a glove or paddle such as a No Miss Velcro® Catch Mitt (Spordas), Sticky Mitt™ or Sticky Monster Mitt™. Alternatively, try catching using a baseball glove or hand paddle.

Objectives:

* to develop the ability to send and receive an object accurately;

* to assess response to form constancy (speed to accommodate different-sized objects);

* to develop tactics for avoidance and interception.

Equipment:

* light footballs – 1 each for half the class;

* tennis balls or small foam balls – up to 4 of each.

Lesson summary

Warm-up: Late for school	5 mins
Vari-catch	5 mins
Beat the bunny	5–10 mins
Falling to bits	5–10 mins
Piggy in the middle	5–10 mins
Cool-down	5 mins
Recap	

NB: Throughout this lesson, emphasise control rather than speed.

Activity	Purpose	Curriculum links: *England* / Scotland

Warm-up: Late for school
 	
◎ Children begin by sitting on the floor. Call out instructions as follows:
 	
    wake up – stand up and stretch;
 	
    jumper on – stretch both arms upwards;
 	
    socks on – balance on left leg, then right leg;
 	
    shoes need fastening – touch toes;
 	
    bus is here – run as fast as possible.
 	
You can add other tasks.
	Stretching and curling in all directions	*1a, 1b, 2b*
		1a, 1b, 2a

Vari-catch
 	
◎ Children get into pairs and stand 2–3m apart. Provide each pair with a light football. They pass the ball to each other:
 	
    underarm;
 	
    overarm;
 	
    with a bounce.
 	
◎ Increase the distance between pairs to 5m.
	Developing aim and catching skills	*1a, 1b, 2b, 2c, 7a*
		2a, 2b, 3a, 3b, 4a

Beat the bunny ◎ Children stand in a large circle (or if the class is large, two smaller circles) with enough space between children to pass a ball. ◎ Introduce 2 balls into the circle: a light football to represent the farmer, a tennis ball or small foam ball for the bunny. Start by passing the bunny, and once this is underway introduce the farmer. The farmer ball moves in the same direction as the bunny ball. ◎ If the 2 balls meet, the bunny is captured, and the child holding the bunny ball is out.	Encouraging rapid accommodation of objects of varying size Changing postural and motor demands to receive different-sized ball A child's appreciation of size (form constancy) can be assessed by observing their response to receiving the balls.	

Activity	Purpose	Curriculum links: *England* / Scotland

Variations

The direction of play may be changed.

Several bunnies may be sent out at the same time.

Several farmers may be introduced.

The bunny and farmer balls may both be bounced on the floor between players.

The distance between players may be widened, according to ability.

1a, 1b, 2b, 2c, 7a, 7b
2a, 3a, 3b, 5a

Falling to bits

◎ Create small circles of approx. 8–10 children. One child stands in the middle of each circle with a light football (choose a child with accurate throwing skills).

◎ This child passes the ball to a player in the circle, who throws it back again. The ball is thrown back and forth round the circle to each child in turn, until it is dropped.

◎ If a child drops the ball, they 'lose a leg' by standing on one leg or by half kneeling. To regain their limb, they must catch the ball 3 times in succession. Further drops, however, result in a loss of:

both legs (full kneeling position is adopted);

an arm (full kneeling position, one arm behind back);

an eye (full kneeling position, one arm behind back, one eye closed).

Variations

Other children can 'earn' limbs for children who have lost one by giving away their 3 consecutive catches.

The central child may also lose body parts.

Motivation to catch is high as playing becomes increasingly difficult when limbs are lost.

1a, 1b, 2b, 2c, 7a
2a, 3a, 3b, 5a

Activity	Purpose	Curriculum links: *England* / Scotland
Piggy in the middle ◎ Children may remain in the same circles as in the previous game, or get into smaller groups. One child – the piggy – stands in the middle. ◎ Children in the circle throw the light football to other players in the circle, trying not to let the pig intercept the ball. When the pig has caught the ball, the child who made that throw takes their place in the middle. ◎ The ball may be bounced, thrown overhead or underarm, or given to another person.	Developing aim and interception skills	*1a, 1b, 2b, 2c, 7a, 7b, 7c* 1a, 2a, 2b, 3a, 3b, 4b, 5a
Cool-down ◎ Gather the children into one large circle; you stand in the middle. Pass the ball to each child, making a comment about their achievements in the lesson – e.g. 'Brilliant catching', 'Fantastic team work', 'Good balancing'. Each time, the child throws the ball back with a response of 'Thank you'.	A calming activity designed to leave children feeling positive about the lesson – which may have been difficult for some	*1a, 1b, 2c* 1b, 2a, 6a

Recap   *3a, 3b, 3c, 4a, 4b*   2a, 6a

- Discuss what determined a successful catch. Discuss force in relation to the speed of the ball.

- Who successfully avoided being the pig in the last game? How was this achieved? Discuss strategies and tactics.

Additional differentiation

- All activities may be performed from a wheelchair or alternative chair. In Falling to bits, you could introduce alternative forfeits, such as crossing legs or putting the tongue out. Ask others in the class to think of forfeits.

- Children with attention or spatial difficulties may be confused about the direction of the ball in Beat the bunny. Help with this by tapping the child on either the left or right shoulder to indicate the direction.

Lesson 7

Throw and catch 2

Objectives:

✳ to develop shoulder-girdle stability;

✳ to develop accurate targeting skills;

✳ to encourage accurate catch by using a slower-moving object.

Equipment:

✳ soft frisbees (e.g. Foam Flyers) – 1 for each child;

✳ hula hoops – 1 each for half of the class;

✳ marking tape or chalk.

Lesson summary

Warm-up: Frisbee frolics	5 mins
Pass and catch	10 mins
Frisbee hoopla	10 mins
Team frisbee	10 mins
Cool-down	5 mins
Recap	

Activity	Purpose · Curriculum links: *England* / Scotland
Warm-up: Frisbee frolics ◎ Each child has a soft frisbee and moves around the room as follows: balancing the frisbee on the head; jumping with the frisbee between the knees; balancing the frisbee on an elbow; balancing the frisbee on the back.	Developing balance *1a, 1b, 2a, 2b, 2c, 7a* 1a, 2a, 2b, 3a
Pass and catch ◎ In pairs, children pass the frisbee to each other, gradually increasing the distance between them to 5m. You may have to demonstrate the movement needed to throw frisbees (similar to a backhand pass in tennis).	Giving practice in backhand flick Developing hand–eye coordination *1a, 1b, 2a, 2b, 2c, 7a* 2a, 2b, 3a, 3b, 5a
Frisbee hoopla ◎ Children work again in pairs. One child holds a hula hoop in a vertical position 2m away from their partner, who attempts to flick the frisbees through the hoop. If successful, they take a step back. Repeat to a distance of 8m away, or closer if it becomes too difficult. ◎ Children change roles.	Developing accurate aim *1a, 1b, 2a, 2b, 2c, 7a* 2a, 2b, 3a, 3b, 5a
Team frisbee ◎ Mark out a small court approximately 12m x 6m. At each end, stand two children holding a hoop in a vertical position as a goal. ◎ Put the children into teams of 6 or 7 players. ◎ Each team tries to score goals by throwing their frisbee through the hoop. Players are not allowed to move with the frisbee and should be encouraged to pass to members of their team.	Throwing and fielding practice

Activity	Purpose	Curriculum links: *England* / Scotland

◎ Once a goal has been scored, the teams change over. The team who scored the most goals throughout the whole competition are the winners.

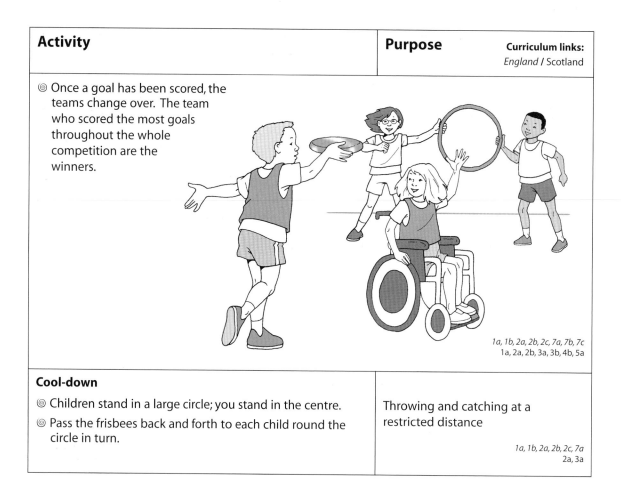

1a, 1b, 2a, 2b, 2c, 7a, 7b, 7c
1a, 2a, 2b, 3a, 3b, 4b, 5a

Cool-down	
◎ Children stand in a large circle; you stand in the centre. ◎ Pass the frisbees back and forth to each child round the circle in turn.	Throwing and catching at a restricted distance
	1a, 1b, 2a, 2b, 2c, 7a *2a, 3a*

Recap   *3a, 3b, 3c, 4a, 4b*   6a

- Discuss the control and effort required to throw the frisbees. Which takes more effort: throwing a frisbee or a tennis ball?

Alternative methods of throwing and catching

Area: *Games*

Objectives:

✱ to develop ball projection;

✱ to develop team cooperation;

✱ to self-regulate upper-limb effort.

Equipment:

✱ beach balls (e.g. Spordas Super Duty Beach Balls™) or large round balloons – 1 for each child;

✱ 6 or 7 throw-and-catch nets (e.g. Spordas Fling-It™) or large towels;

✱ 1 goal (e.g Giant Go 4 Goal™) or a hula hoop or empty storage container;

✱ marking tape or chalk;

✱ stopwatch or egg timer;

✱ CD player and soft music (e.g. the theme from *Robinson Crusoe* by Art of Noise or 'Equinox' by Jean-Michel Jarre).

Lesson summary

Warm-up: Move to the beat	5 mins
Moon ball	5 mins
Beach ball flick	10 mins
Throw, flick and catch	10 mins
Target flick	10 mins
Cool-down	5 mins
Recap	

Activity	Purpose	Curriculum links: *England* / Scotland
Warm-up: Move to the beat ◎ Children run around the room in various directions and speeds, as you direct. Alter the plane of movement from high to low. ◎ Create a rhythm by clapping; children move according to the rhythm, incorporating stretches and tucks.	Gently warming up the body in anticipation of action	*1b, 2a, 8a* 1a, 1b, 2a
Moon ball ◎ Gather the whole class in the centre of room, pat a beach ball or balloon into the air, and ask them to attempt to keep it airborne for as long as possible, using either hand. Together, count the number of hits before the ball falls to the ground.	Warming-up activity which emphasises hand–eye coordination	*1a, 1b, 2b, 2c, 7a* 1a, 2a, 2b, 3a
Beach ball flick ◎ Put children into groups of 4. ◎ Provide each group with a throw-and-catch net (or large towel). Each child holds a corner. Place a beach ball in the centre. They flick the ball up and catch it in the net. Encourage them to see how high they can toss the ball.	Encouraging cooperation and negotiation skills, and self-regulation of effort You may wish to use this activity to assess the children's leadership skills.	*1a, 1b, 2b, 2c, 7a, 7b* 3a, 5a

Activity	Purpose	Curriculum links: *England / Scotland*

Throw, flick and catch

◎ Staying in the same groups, two children hold the net at the corners while the other two stand either side of it, one holding the ball.

◎ The child with the beach ball throws it onto the net. As the ball lands, the net holders flick it across to be caught by the catcher on the opposite side. This will require a twisting motion to catch and direct the ball simultaneously.

◎ Following several attempts, change positions so that all children have a go at throwing, flicking and catching.

◎ If towels are used and the towel is too large for two children to hold, either fold it in half, or use smaller towels for this activity.

This game will only be successful with coordinated movements of the towel; this will require close cooperation between all team members and accurate timing of actions.

1a, 1b, 2b, 2c, 7a, 7b
2a, 3a, 3b, 5a

Target flick

◎ Children remain in the same groups, to compete in teams of 4.

◎ Set up a goal by positioning a Giant Go 4 Goal™ or have two children not in a group hold a hula hoop or empty storage container in a horizontal position at shoulder level. Draw a line 3–4m away from the goal.

◎ Two children stand on the line holding the throw-and catch net or towel; the other two act as runners.

◎ Each team has 3 minutes to stand on the target line and flick the beach ball into the target.

The runners must return the ball to the net so that further attempts can be made within the 3-minute period.

◎ If the class is large, provide a second goal and have two teams competing at one time.

Developing coordinated movement and flicking motion, and spatial organisation

1a, 1b, 2b, 2c, 7a, 7b
1a, 2a, 2b, 3a, 3b, 4b, 5a

Cool-down

◎ Play some soft music. In pairs, the children hold the nets, with a hand at each corner. Together, they create a sequence incorporating slow movements in various directions as well as twists and turns.

Calming activity

1a, 1b, 2b, 2c, 2a, 2b
4a, 5a, 5b

© Get Physical! LDA   Permission to Photocopy

Recap   *3a, 3b, 3c, 4a, 4b*   *5a, 6a*

- Discuss how today's lesson demonstrated ways to project a ball other than with hands or with a bat. Can the class think of any more ways in which objects can be propelled? Refer to science relating to forces and movement.

- Discuss the importance of working together to succeed in these tasks. Each person is different – i.e. in height, weight and ability – but all have a part.

Additional differentiation

- If upper-limb function is restricted, encourage bilateral hand skills whenever possible, intertwining the fingers of both hands with the net.

- Children with ADHD may flick the net erratically because of their poor movement awareness and fleeting attention. Provide these children with a larger net or towel; the increased effort required should increase control.

Preparation for bat and ball skills

Area: *Games*

Objectives:

❋ to develop spatial planning and organisation;

❋ to adjust effort of strike according to distance;

❋ to develop accurate hand–eye coordination.

Equipment:

❋ beach balls (e.g. Spordas Super Duty Beach Balls™) or large round balloons – 1 for each child;

❋ marking tape or chalk;

❋ a volleyball net or Qwik Net™.

Children could inflate the balloons before the lesson. Ensure that a few extra are available, in case any burst.

Lesson summary

Warm-up: Simon says	5 mins
Beach ball balance	5 mins
Beach ball pat and shift	5 mins
Circle pass	5 mins
Beach ball volleyball	10 mins
Cool-down	5 mins
Recap	

Activity	Purpose	Curriculum links: *England* / Scotland
Warm-up: Simon says ◎ Play a game of Simon says. Incorporate stretching upwards, touching the toes, leaning sideways, and moving the head forwards and backwards, and from side to side.	Warming up muscles, particularly those surrounding the shoulder girdle	
		1a, 1b, 2b, 2c 1a, 1b, 2a
Beach ball balance ◎ Give each child a beach ball (or balloon). ◎ Children pat the ball up in the air with their hands continuously, without its falling to the ground. They could count the number of pats before the ball falls.	Appreciating the speed of movement Using the beach ball allows more time to assess distance and time between object and contact.	
		1a, 1b, 2b, 7a 2a, 3a, 3b
Beach ball pat and shift ◎ Children get into pairs. Pairs stand in a row down the middle of the room, with the children in each pair facing each other, approx. 1m apart. Each pair has a beach ball (or balloon). ◎ Pairs pat the ball backwards and forwards to each other. After 3 successful passes, they each step back 0.5m. They continue until they are 4–5m apart.	Developing accurate hand–eye coordination Appreciating spatial relationships	
		1a, 1b, 2a, 2b, 7a 2a, 2b, 3a, 3b, 5a
Circle pass ◎ Children stand in a circle; you stand in the middle. Pat the ball (or balloon) to each child and back again, moving around the circle. The ball should be kept in continuous motion. ◎ Anticipation may be incorporated by passing the ball to children selected at random.	Developing anticipation and coordinated strike	
		1a, 1b, 2a, 2b, 2c, 7a 2a, 3a, 3b, 6a

Activity	Purpose	Curriculum links: *England* / Scotland

Beach ball volleyball

◎ Mark out a basic mini-volleyball court 12m x 6m and put up a 6m-wide volleyball net halfway across. The net should be approximately 155cm high.

◎ Put the class into teams of approx. 6.

◎ Play a simplified version of volleyball, with rules as follows:

Developing group cooperation; hand–eye coordination

Propulsion uses upper-limb effort and stamina.

> The aim of the game is to pat the ball over the net to land on your opponents' court.
>
> Each time the ball hits the floor the other team get a point.
>
> The first team to get 10 points are the winners.
>
> Each team are entitled to a maximum of 3 passes before the ball is sent over the net.
>
> You must keep the ball inside the court area.

◎ Explain that instead of volleyballs, which are quite heavy and hard, you are using beach balls (or balloons), which will call for extra effort to get them across the net.

1a, 1b, 2a, 2b, 2c, 7a, 7b, 7c
1a, 3a, 3b, 4b, 5a, 6a

Cool-down

◎ Children stand in a space. They close their eyes, stretch up as high as possible, then hold and count to 5. Then they lower arms slowly, move down to a crouch on the floor, hold the position and count to 5.

◎ Repeat 4 times.

Stretching and calming muscles

1a, 1b
1a, 1b

Recap   *3a, 3b, 3c, 4a, 4b   6a*

● Discuss how much effort was required when hitting a beach ball (or balloon) rather than a football. Discuss in relation to 'effort' in science.

● What were the advantages of using the lighter ball? What were the disadvantages?

Additional differentiation

● Beach ball volleyball can be adapted further by asking all children to play seated on chairs with the net lowered.

Objectives:

✽ to develop successful hand–eye coordination;

✽ to encourage accurate assessment of space and speed;

✽ to develop effective strike action.

Equipment:

✽ small paddle bats, or short-handled rackets – 1 for each child;

✽ balloons – 1 each for half the class;

✽ 2–4 low nets (e.g. Qwik Net™);

✽ marking tape or chalk.

Children could inflate the balloons before the lesson. Ensure that a few extra are available in case of bursts.

Lesson summary

Warm-up: Mirror moves	5 mins
Bat and pat	10 mins
Balloon bat	10 mins
Balloon tennis	10 mins
Cool-down	5 mins
Recap	

Activity	Purpose **Curriculum links:** *England* / Scotland
Warm-up: Mirror moves ◎ Children run around the room, altering direction and speed as you direct. ◎ Children get into pairs and face each other. One creates a series of movements which involves stretches and actions in a variety of planes; the other copies the sequence. ◎ Change leaders.	Encouraging accurate observation while warming up muscles *1a, 1b, 2a, 2b, 6b* 1a, 2a, 3a, 3b, 5b
Bat and pat ◎ Children get into pairs. Provide one child in each pair with a paddle bat (or short-handled racket) and the other with a balloon. ◎ Pairs practise passing the balloon backwards and forwards, with one child using a flat palm and the other using a bat. ◎ After 5 minutes change over, so that both children have an opportunity to use the bat.	Encouraging children to appreciate the speed at which a balloon travels in order to achieve success with hand–eye coordination *1a, 1b, 2b, 2c, 7a* 2a, 2b, 3a, 3b, 5a, 5b
Balloon bat ◎ Put up 2 or 3 low 6m nets (or mark a line). Provide each child with a paddle bat (or short-handled racket). ◎ When children have got into pairs, give each pair a balloon and allocate several pairs to work at each net. ◎ Children pat their balloons to each other across the net or central line, using the bats. They can see how many times they can bat the balloon across and back without it falling to the ground.	Encouraging controlled strike of the balloon with bat *1a, 1b, 2b, 2c, 7a, 7b* 2a, 3a, 3b, 4b, 5a, 5b, 6a

Activity	Purpose	Curriculum links: *England* / Scotland

Balloon tennis

◉ Using marking tape or chalk, create up to 4 mini-tennis courts, each 4m x 8m. Put up a low net on each court.

◉ In groups of 4, children play a game of adapted mixed doubles, by passing the balloon over the net with their bat. A scorer can be allocated for each team, but they must also have an opportunity to play a game. Rules are as follows:

  If the balloon hits the floor, the opposing team get a point.

  The balloon must stay inside the court area.

  The first team to score 10 points are the winners.

Developing controlled hand–eye coordination and assessment of effort through upper limbs

1a, 1b, 2b, 2c, 7a, 7b, 7c
2a, 3a, 3b, 4b, 4c, 5a

Cool-down

◉ Children sit on the floor in pairs, facing each other and holding hands. They sing 'Row, row, row your boat', gently and slowly rocking forwards and back while singing.

◉ In the same position, they rock slowly from side to side, singing 'The big ship sails on the alley, alley, O'.

Calming activity

1a, 2b
1b, 2a, 5a

Recap *3a, 3b, 3c, 4a, 4b*   *6a*

• What did the children need to do to make the balloons travel a greater distance?

Objectives:

✳ to develop hand–eye coordination;

✳ to encourage accurate assessment of space and speed;

✳ to improve response times.

Equipment:

✳ small paddle bats or short-handled rackets – 1 for each child;

✳ soft balls or shuttlecocks –1 each for half of the class;

✳ some low nets (e.g. Qwik Net™) or marking tape or chalk;

✳ cricket stumps (either indoor or outdoor);

✳ 1 soft baseball bat.

Lesson summary

Warm-up: Sing and stretch	5 mins
Round the wheel	5 mins
Back to you	5 mins
Softball tennis	5–10 mins
(or short-bat badminton)	
Crocker	10 mins
Cool-down	5 mins

Activity	Purpose	Curriculum links: *England I Scotland*
Warm-up: Sing and stretch ◎ Sing some group songs which require stretching actions, such as 'The hokey-cokey' and 'Heads and shoulders, knees and toes' (varying the speed). ◎ Conclude with a Mexican wave.	Stretching the muscles in preparation for bat and ball activities	*1a, 2b* 1a, 1b, 3c, 5a
Round the wheel ◎ Children stand in a large circle (or if the class is large and you have some adult assistance, two smaller circles). You stand in the middle holding a small paddle bat (or short-handled racket). ◎ One child throws a soft ball (or shuttlecock) to you, and you bat it to the next child to catch. Carry on throwing and batting around the circle.	Introducing children to the level of control needed to hit the ball back to a specific target	*1a, 1b, 2b, 2c, 7a* 2a, 2b, 3a, 3b, 5a
Back to you ◎ Children get into pairs. Give one child a paddle bat (or short-handled racket) and the other a soft ball (or shuttlecock). ◎ Children start 2m apart. The first child throws the ball, their partner bats it back, and the first child catches it. They continue, alternating the batter and gradually increasing the distance between them up to 5m. ◎ An element of competition may be added by asking pairs to count how many times they can bat and catch without the ball falling to the ground.	Developing effective targeting and hand–eye coordination	*1a, 1b, 2b, 2c, 7b* 2a, 2b, 3a, 3b, 5a, 5b
Softball tennis (or short-bat badminton) ◎ Set up a series of low nets (or mark lines on floor). Provide each child with a small paddle bat (or short-handled racket).	Developing hand–eye coordination	

Activity	Purpose	Curriculum links: *England / Scotland*

◎ In pairs, the children bat the soft ball (or shuttlecock) to each other either across the net. Encourage them to count how many times they can pass the ball without it falling to the floor.

1a, 1b, 2b, 2c, 7a, 7b, 7c
2a, 2b, 3a, 3b, 4b, 5a, 5b

Crocker (non-stop cricket)

◎ Put the class into two teams; one to field first and the other to bat first.

◎ Position cricket stumps centrally and place a further single stump 3m away horizontally.

◎ The first child stands in front of, but not obstructing, the stumps, and the bowler (positioned 4m in front of batter) bowls the ball. It is important to appoint a good bowler for this game to be successful.

◎ The batter attempts to hit the ball with the soft baseball bat, then runs around the single stump and returns to their original position. Even if the ball is not hit, the batter must run. They should run as many times around the route as possible: the more runs, the more points for their team.

◎ The bowler must try to hit the stumps. As soon as the stumps are knocked over, or the ball is caught, the batter is out, and another rushes to take their place. The bowler may continue to bowl even if the stumps are unguarded. Play continues until all the batting team are out.

◎ The fielding team must field well to get each player out as quickly as possible. If the ball is caught 3 times by the fielding team, the whole team is out.

A competitive game in which each child has an opportunity to hit the ball with the bat (although this is not essential for the success of the game)

Providing the opportunity for defence and attacking tactics, and for teamwork

1a, 1b, 2b, 2c, 7a, 7b, 7c
2a, 2b, 3a, 3b, 4a, 4b, 4c, 5a, 5b

Cool-down

◎ Children stand in a space. They bend down to touch their toes, then slowly stretch up, inhaling deeply in the process. They exhale slowly as they bend to touch their toes again.

◎ Repeat 5 times.

Calming activity

1a, 1b
1b, 2a

Recap *3a, 3b, 3c, 4a, 4b*   *5a, 6a*

- Think about the game of Crocker. What was important in making the game successful? (Everyone participating, everyone encouraging each other, a sense of competition, and the speed of the game.) What would have happened if the fielders had given up passing the ball? Stress the fact that this game relies on everyone staying interested and committed to their team.

- Relate this back to corporate reward schemes which may be running in the school.

Additional differentiation

- If a child is unable to strike a moving object, help them to practise their strike using a batting tee such as the Up Rite Safe Tee. Alternatively, position the ball on top of a tall cone.

- Another way to help children with hand–eye coordination difficulties is to acquire a batting trainer or swing ball to help them accommodate a moving object.

Lesson 12   Bat and ball skills 3

Area: *Games*

Objectives:

✳ to develop laterality;

✳ to encourage crossing of the body's midline;

✳ to expand bilateral hand–eye coordination.

Equipment:

✳ 4 large foam balls;

✳ 16 cones;

✳ old newspaper to make small newspaper batons –
2 for each child;

✳ marking tape or chalk;

✳ coloured tabards or team bands.

Newspaper batons may be made in class by the children
before the lesson.

Lesson summary

Warm-up: Scissors	5 mins
Crazy walks	5 mins
Human slalom	5 mins
Hockey slalom	5–10 mins
Two-handed hockey	10 mins
Cool-down	5 mins
Recap	

Activity	Purpose	Curriculum links: *England* **/** Scotland

Warm-up: Scissors

◉ Children do 5 each of the following:

  star jumps;

  stretch and touch toe with opposite hand,
  keeping legs straight;

  scissor jumps (jump and land with legs apart,
  then jump and land with legs crossed);

  knee lifts with left hand touching right
  knee, alternating with right hand touching
  left knee;

  cross-standing: standing up from sitting
  cross-legged on floor (to make this harder,
  stand up with arms crossed as well).

Scissor jumps

Warming up muscles and
encouraging midline crossing

1a, 1b, 2a, 2b
1a, 1b, 2a

Crazy walks

◉ Create some imaginary creatures
that crawl and walk with legs
and arms crossing and
uncrossing. Children
demonstrate how these
creatures would move
around the room.

Encouraging reciprocal crawling but
with exaggerated crossing of the
midline

1a, 1b, 2a, 2b
2a, 2b, 3a, 4a

Activity	Purpose	Curriculum links: *England* / Scotland
Human slalom	Developing hand–eye coordination and ball control	
◉ Put the class into 4 teams. The teams stand in parallel lines across the room, with a space of approx. 1m between team members.		
◉ Using a crawling or crouching position, the first member of each team must gently push a large foam ball down the length of the team, weaving in and out between the team members and using alternate hands to control the ball. The ball should not lift from the floor.		
◉ On reaching the opposite wall, they carry the ball back to the next player, who will repeat the process. The first team member goes to the end of the line and the rest of the team shuffle down to reposition the slalom.		
◉ The first team to finish are the winners.	*1a, 1b, 2b, 2c, 7a, 7c* 1a, 2a, 2b, 3a, 3b, 4c, 5a	
Hockey slalom	Developing hand–eye coordination	
◉ Children stay in the same teams.		
◉ This time, create a slalom course with a line of 4 cones per team. Provide each child with two newspaper batons, one for each hand.		
◉ The first team member dribbles a large foam ball in and out of the cones to the opposite side of the room.		
◉ When they reach the opposite wall, they carry the ball back to the next player, who repeats the process.		
◉ The first team to finish are the winners.	*1a, 1b, 2b, 2c, 7a, 7b, 7c* 1a, 2a, 2b, 3a, 3b, 4c, 5a	
Two-handed hockey	Developing bilateral coordination	
◉ Mark out a 12m x 6m hockey pitch with a central dividing line, so each side is 6m x 6m. Set up two goals using cones 1.5m apart.		
◉ Create teams of 6–8 players, identifying each team using coloured tabards or team bands. Each child has two newspaper batons, one for each hand.		
◉ Children play a simplified game of hockey, using the newspaper batons as sticks and a large foam ball.		
◉ Players bat the ball along the floor, and pass wherever possible to other team members with the aim of reaching the opposition's goal and scoring.	*1a, 1b, 2b, 2c, 7a, 7b, 7c* 1a, 2a, 2b, 3a, 3b, 4a, 4b, 5a	

Activity	Purpose	Curriculum links: *England / Scotland*
Cool-down ◉ In a circle, sing songs with actions which incorporate reciprocal movements of the arms and legs and incorporate crossing the midline, e.g. 'The hokey-cokey', 'Macarena', 'Pat-a-cake', 'If you're happy and you know it ...' (adding complex actions, such as folding your arms).	Calming activities which include bilateral and crossed-midline actions	*1a, 1b, 2b, 2c* *1b, 2a, 3b*

Recap   *3a, 3b, 3c, 4a, 4b*   *5b, 6a*

- Discuss laterality with children, explaining that most people use either their left or right hand to write and draw, and use the leg on the same side to lead an activity such as marching, climbing or kicking. Do a mini-survey to demonstrate which children are left/right handed.

  Make a note of any child who is unsure which hand they regularly use, or if it is evident that the child has confused laterality (i.e. they use the opposite hand and eye). Make a note also of children who appear to struggle to cross their arms over the midline position.

- Children with laterality confusion and those who cannot cross the midline are at risk of motor coordination difficulties, which will particularly affect handwriting and bilateral activities such as cutting with scissors, craft work and practical maths.

- Ask children to observe which hand is used the most by members of their family, and use the details in maths lessons to make a graph.

Additional differentiation

- Children who have limited use of one side of their body should be encouraged to bring both arms together by interlocking fingers in a midline position; an arm gaiter may be needed to maintain the affected arm in an extended (straight) position.

- Many children will be unsure about which hand is their left and which right. A distinguishing feature such as a mole, birthmark or scar may help the child to work out left and right. Alternatively a sticker could be placed on one hand.

Object transfer 1

Area: *Games*

Objectives:

✳ to develop bimanual coordination;

✳ to develop midline orientation;

✳ to extend shoulder-girdle stability.

Equipment:

✳ 4 beanbags;

✳ marking tape or chalk;

✳ cardboard fish, approx. length 25cm – 1 for each child;

✳ tabloid-size newspapers folded to approx. A4 – 1 for each child.

The fish may be made by children before the PE lesson.

Lesson summary

Warm-up: Glue	5 mins
Stuck-mitts	10 mins
Flap-a-fish	10 mins
Fish o' war	10 mins
Cool-down	5 mins
Recap	

Activity	Purpose	Curriculum links: *England* **/** Scotland
Warm-up: Glue ◉ One child – the catcher – stands in the centre of the room. The rest of the class must attempt to cross the room without being caught. When a child is caught, they join hands with the catcher and together they carry on catching. As others are caught, they join onto the chain. ◉ The chain must stay connected until everyone has been caught.	Warming up muscles	*1a, 2b* 1a, 1b, 2a, 2b

Stuck-mitts
 	
◉ Put the class into 4 teams. The teams stand in parallel lines across the room, with a space of approx. 1m between team members.
 	
◉ Ask children to intertwine fingers and imagine that they have accidentally got superglue onto their fingers, and their hands are now stuck together.
 	
◉ The teams have to race to pass a beanbag along from one to another, keeping fingers interlocked so that only the palms are used to grip the object. If any fingers become loose, the team is disqualified.
 	
Variations
 	
◉ Pass the beanbag:
      over the head;
      under the legs;
      to the left;
      to the right;
      through the legs and over the head alternately.
	Developing bimanual, symmetrical coordination and the ability to cross the midline
	
	This game forces children to use both hands together.
		1a, 1b, 2b, 2c, 7a
		2a, 3a, 3b, 5a, 5b

Activity	Purpose	Curriculum links: *England* / Scotland
Flap-a-fish ◎ Children stay in the same teams. ◎ Each team has a folded newspaper (the flapper) and each child has a cardboard fish. Curl the fishes' noses and tails up slightly. ◎ The first child in each team wafts the fish across the room by flapping the newspaper behind it, holding with both hands. As soon as they reach the finishing line, they rush back to their team and pass on the flapper so that the next team member can start. The first team to get all their fishes across are the winners.	Developing bimanual symmetrical gross motor arm movements Enhancing shoulder-girdle stability	*1a, 1b, 2b, 2c, 7a* 2a, 3a, 5a, 5b
Fish o' war ◎ Draw a cross in the centre of the room. At either side, approx. 1.5m away, draw a horizontal line. ◎ Put children into teams of 4 and give each child a newspaper flapper. Each team should stand behind their respective line, looking towards the fish which is placed centrally on the cross. ◎ On the word 'Go', each team must try to flap their fish over their opponent's line. Children must hold their newspaper flappers with both hands. ◎ The winners are the first team to flap the fish over their opponents' starting line.	Demanding rapid bilateral upper-limb movements	*1a, 1b, 2b, 2c, 7a, 7b* 2a, 3a, 3b, 4b, 5a
Cool-down ◎ Children find a space to lie on the floor on their backs. They intertwine their fingers, raise their arms above their head, stretch their arms and legs, then hold and count to 5 seconds. ◎ They attempt to sit up with hands still together (using abdominal muscles), then slowly recline again. Repeat 3 times.	Retaining midline orientation, control extension and flexion using muscles of the trunk	*1a, 1b, 2b* 1b, 2a

Recap   *3b, 3c, 4a, 4b*   3a, 6a

- Discuss the fact that today's session required symmetrical arm movement. Can children think of other activities where both arms have to work together symmetrically? (Consider swimming (breast-stroke), rowing, steering a go-cart, clapping, and gymnastics.)

- Relate the lesson to the introduction of symmetry in Key Stage 1 numeracy lessons – space and shape section.

Object transfer 2

Objectives:

✳ to encourage pressure through the upper limbs;

✳ to develop bilateral control and reciprocal action;

✳ to increase shoulder strength.

Equipment:

✳ marking tape or chalk;

✳ 4 or 5 scooterboards (e.g. Spordas Megascoots™) or skateboards (ask some children to bring theirs in for this lesson);

✳ beanbags;

✳ 2 large buckets.

Lesson summary

Warm-up: Creepy crawlies	5 mins
Scooter transfer	5–10 mins
Scooter pick-up and drop	5–10 mins
Speedy snails	5–10 mins
Cool-down	5 mins
Recap	

Activity	Purpose	Curriculum links: *England / Scotland*
Warm-up: Creepy crawlies ◎ Children cross the room using various types of crawling position, e.g.: Commando crawl – move opposite arms and legs. Slithery snake – keep legs together and use a slithering movement to slide across the floor, using arms to pull. Caterpillar creep – keep legs together, bend them up towards the stomach, while at the same time stretching arms out, then extend legs to move forwards (like a caterpillar). Spider shuffle – creep sideways, balancing on knees and extended arms.	Developing reciprocal use of arms and legs	

1a, 1b, 2a, 2b
1a, 2a, 2b, 3b

Activity	Purpose	Curriculum links: *England* / Scotland

Scooter transfer

◎ Put the class into 4 or 5 teams.

◎ Mark a starting line. All teams line up behind it. At the front of each team, behind the line, are a scooterboard (or skateboard) and several beanbags; opposite the team on the other side of the room is a bucket.

◎ The first child lies on the scooterboard, picks up a beanbag, tucks it between the scooterboard and their chest, and scoots across the room, using their hands. When they reach the bucket, they drop the beanbag in, jump off the scooterboard, then run back with it to give to the next person in their team.

◎ Do a practice run before racing competitively.

◎ Remind the children to keep their fingers away from the wheels.

Developing shoulder stability

Stimulating joint position sense

1a, 2b, 7a
1a, 2a, 2b, 3a, 3b, 4c, 5a

Scooter pick-up and drop

◎ Put the class into teams of approx. 8.

◎ Line up the teams alongside each other across the room, with half of each team at one side and the other half positioned opposite. Place two buckets between each pair of teams and place a beanbag inside each bucket.

◎ The first child in each team lies on a scooterboard, scoots to their first bucket and collects the beanbag, proceeds to the second bucket and collects the beanbag, then continues to the opposite side of the room. The first team member on that side of the room lies on the skateboard and scoots back, returning a beanbag to each bucket on the way.

Developing kinaesthetic sense by applying pressure through the upper limbs

Developing hand–eye coordination

◎ Continue until all team members have crossed the room.

◎ Do a practice run before racing competitively.

1a, 1b, 2a, 2b, 7a, 7b
1a, 2a, 3a, 3b, 4b, 4c, 5a, 6a

Activity	Purpose	Curriculum links: *England* / Scotland
Speedy snails	Developing kinaesthetic sense	
◎ Children stay in the same teams and get into pairs. One will be the pusher, the other the snail (the snail's house will be a strategically placed beanbag). Place a bucket opposite each team on the other side of the room.		
◎ The first snail lies on a scooterboard (or skateboard), with the beanbag placed centrally on their back. The pusher holds the snail's feet and pushes them across the hall.		
◎ On reaching the other side, they put the beanbag into the bucket. Both children run back and give the scooterboard to the next pair, whose turn it is to be a speedy snail.		
◎ If a child falls off the board, the pair are disqualified, so care must be taken to ensure the snail remains balanced.		
◎ Do a practice run before racing competitively.		
◎ Extend the game by having the pusher pulling the snail back again.		*1a, 1b, 2a, 2b, 7a, 7b* 1a, 2a, 3a, 3b, 4b, 4c, 5a, 6a
Cool-down	Revisiting the positions used in today's lesson, in a calm, controlled manner	
◎ Create a series of mini-beast positions which involve curling and stretching, e.g.: snail – curl up in a ball, tummy towards the floor; worm – stretch out with tummy on the floor; caterpillar – create an arch either forwards or backwards; ladybird – curl up tight with back on floor.		
◎ Randomly call out the names of the mini-beasts. Each time, children hold the pose for 5 seconds. Encourage accurate positioning.		
◎ At the end of the session, shout 'Seagull coming!' In response, the children must escape to one side of the room as fast as possible.		*1a, 1b, 2b* 1b, 2a, 3b

Recap   *3a, 3b, 3c, 4a, 4b*   1b, 2a, 6a

- Discuss the importance of crawling in order to develop strength in the shoulders and arms. This helps to increase stability at the shoulders and subsequently improve control of hand function.

- Strength in the arms helps to push and pull objects. Give examples of pushing activities: supermarket trolley, scooters, Play-Doh, etc. Ask for further examples and for ones that involve pulling. Is it easier to push or pull?

Additional differentiation

- Independent scooting may not be possible for children with restricted upper-limb function, but being pushed on a scooter by another person will provide essential vestibular stimulation.

- Children who have unilateral upper-limb function will need guidance to ensure that the scooterboard follows a straight line, as asymmetry will affect the direction of movement.

Lesson 15 Object transfer 3

Area: *Games*

Objectives:

- to develop cooperation and teamwork;
- to enhance motor planning and organisation;
- to create alternative motor strategies.

Equipment:

- 2 footballs;
- marking tape or chalk;
- 24 beanbags;
- 4 or 5 large foam balls;
- large gym mats – 2 between 4 children.

Lesson summary

Warm-up: Over, through, across	5 mins
Cooperative beanbag relay	10 mins
Handless ball relay	10 mins
Escaping pirates	10 mins
Cool-down	5 mins
Recap	

Activity	Purpose	Curriculum links: *England* / Scotland

Warm-up: Over, through, across

Children sit on the floor in a large circle (or two smaller circles, if the class is large). Pass two footballs around the circle in the following ways:

over the head;

through the legs (under knees);

using the feet and no hands.

Purpose: Exploring ways of passing a ball while warming up muscles through controlled stretches

1a, 1b, 2a, 2b, 2c, 7a
1a, 1b, 2a, 3a, 4a, 4b

Activity	Purpose	Curriculum links: *England / Scotland*
Cooperative beanbag relay	Developing teamwork Increasing proprioceptive feedback	
◎ Put the class into teams of 6. Mark a starting line and a finishing line. Teams line up behind the start. Only 2 teams will move at a time.		
◎ Explain that each race involves working together to transport a set of beanbags from the start to the finishing line. A total of 3 beanbags must be transferred during each race – which may require several journeys across the room.		

◎ Teams race in the following ways:
    Piggy back – one child carried on another's back.
    Fireman's lift – two children hold hands, a further child sits on the 'seat' made with their hands.
    Hopping rabbit – in pairs, children must support each other to balance, with one child using their left leg, the other their right, together hopping across.
    Wheelbarrow – one child holds the thighs of the other, who moves forwards balancing on arms only.		

Children can be creative about how they balance the beanbag.	*1a, 1b, 2a, 2b, 2c, 7a* *1a, 2a, 2b, 3a, 3b, 5a*	
Handless ball relay	Developing teamwork, motor planning and organisation	
◎ Children stay in the same teams and get into pairs. Give each team a large foam ball.		

◎ Children must travel from the start to the finish line with the ball, without using their hands. On reaching the finish line, the pair rush back to give the ball to the next pair in their team. Attempt the following:
    no hands;
    no hands, no touching the ground;
    no hands or tummies, no touching the ground;
    back to back;
    no hands and only two feet touching the ground.		

◎ See if the children can suggest other ways of transporting the ball.	*1a, 1b, 2a, 2b, 2c, 7a, 7c* *1a, 2a, 2b, 3a, 3b, 5a, 5b*	
Escaping pirates	Developing negotiation skills, coordination and balance	
◎ This game may be undertaken in the same teams as in the previous game, or the class may be regrouped into teams of 4.		
◎ Each team is given 2 large gym mats (islands) and 3 beanbags (the treasure).		

Activity	**Purpose**	**Curriculum links:** *England* / Scotland
◎ Each team has to cross the room carrying their treasure, standing only on the islands. This will involve a stepping stone action: each team stands on one of their islands, then moves the spare mat ahead and transfers the treasure onto that mat. They then step onto the mat in front and move the mat they have just vacated ahead – and so on until they have crossed the room. ◎ Any team caught stepping on the floor are disqualified.		*1a, 1b, 2a, 2b, 2c, 7a, 7b, 7c* *1a, 3a, 4b, 5a, 5b*
Cool-down ◎ Each team lies on their island, with their eyes closed. Each child thinks of a treasure (their most treasured possession). ◎ Randomly select children to tell everyone what their treasure is. After each suggestion, all the children curl up in a ball as though they are hugging the treasure, then release again.	Flexion and extension stretches, relaxing muscles	*1a, 1b, 2a, 2b, 2c* *1b, 2a*

Recap   *3a, 3b, 3c, 4a, 4b*   5a, 6a

- Discuss the importance of teamwork in today's lesson. How were decisions reached? Did any group have a definite leader? Were there any frustrations?
- On what basis were certain roles selected? Who decided who should be carried and who should carry during the piggy-back race?

Additional differentiation

- In Cooperative beanbag relay, children whose mobility is impaired may be carried for the piggy-back race and fireman's lift. Children with limited strength in their upper limbs may struggle to maintain a wheelbarrow position. Allow them to travel bearing their weight through their elbows rather than their hands.

Objectives:

❋ to develop cooperative teamwork;

❋ to enhance joint position sense (proprioception) by increasing effort through the upper and lower limbs;

❋ to increase tactile sensation and therefore enhance self-awareness (body schema).

Equipment:

❋ 4–6 large foam balls or footballs;

❋ 2 cones;

❋ plastic indoor hockey sticks (the Hok-E-Stik™ set by Davies Sport provides variable handle lengths so they can be adapted according to ability) or 1.5m lengths of narrow plastic pipe;

❋ marking tape or chalk;

❋ crepe bandages or scarves.

Lesson summary

Warm-up: Beans	5 mins
Dribble ball	5–10 mins
Foosball	10 mins
Three-legged football dribble	10 mins
Cool-down	5 mins
Recap	

Activity	Purpose **Curriculum links:** *England* / Scotland

Warm-up: Beans
 	
◎ Children move according to the type of bean called:
 	
    jumping beans – jump on spot;
    runner beans – run around room;
    broad beans – large strides with arms horizontal;
    jelly beans – wobbly walk;
    frozen beans – stand still;
    bean sprout – stretch up tall and walk on tiptoes;
    has beans! – lie flat out on floor.
	Warming up muscles with resistance being given by working in pairs
	
	1a, 1b, 2a, 2b
	1a, 1b, 2a, 5a

Dribble ball ◎ Put the children in teams of 4 and give a foam ball (or football) to each team. ◎ Team members take turns to dribble their ball across the room, using alternate feet. On reaching the opposite side of the room, the ball must be picked up and returned to the next team member. ◎ Extend the activity by placing a cone at the end of the room opposite each team. Team members take turns to dribble a ball, using alternate feet. They travel across the room, round the cone and back to the team.	Developing foot–eye coordination *1a, 1b, 2b, 2c, 7b, 7c* 2a, 3a, 3b, 5a

Activity	Purpose	Curriculum links: *England* / Scotland

Foosball

Table football – with real players.

◉ Put the class into 2 or 4 opposing teams. Each team forms two or three rows of 3 or 4 children. The teams face each other in alternate rows.

◉ At each end, 2 cones are placed as goals, and one child from each team goes in goal.

◉ Each child in a row holds the end of an indoor hockey stick (or length of plastic pipe) in each hand (those on the ends of rows will hold only one end) so that each row is joined up.

Developing skills for simple strike and invasion games, and team skills

◉ A foam ball (or football) is rolled into the game to start play. Each team must try to kick the ball into their goal; this will require passing the ball forwards or backwards. Children must retain their grip on their stick and can only move left or right to kick the ball. They must not move forwards or backwards.

◉ If the class is in 4 teams, swap teams.

1a, 1b, 2b, 2c, 7b, 7c
3a, 4b, 5a, 6a

Three-legged football dribble

◉ Mark a starting and a finishing line. Children get into pairs. Each pair is joined loosely at the ankles with a crepe bandage (or scarf) – as for a 3-legged race.

◉ Put the pairs into 4 teams. Give a foam ball (or football) to each team. Each pair in turn attempts to dribble the ball from a starting line to a finish line. Success depends on control and negotiation rather than speed. When they reach the line, they bring the ball back for the next pair.

Encouraging coordinated movements

Developing leadership and team-building skills

1a, 1b, 2b, 2c, 7c
3a, 3b, 5a, 5b

Activity	Purpose	Curriculum links: *England* / Scotland
Cool-down ◎ Remaining in pairs, the children face each other and place their palms together so that their hands are pointing the same way. Both children close their eyes. ◎ One child leads by slowly moving their hands in various directions; the other child must maintain contact and mirror the actions. ◎ Swap leaders and repeat. Encourage variations in direction demanding whole-body involvement.	Calming activity which continues to demand contact with others	*1a, 1b, 2b* *4a, 5a, 5b*

Recap   *3a, 3b, 3c, 4a, 4b*   *5a, 5b, 6a*

- Explore how easy or difficult it was to move when you were joined to another person. What was frustrating? How did you decide which direction to take? (Explain the importance of shared decision-making.)

Additional differentiation

- Support children who have restricted mobility at the hips to sit independently on a stool. Movement will be restricted, but in this position the child can kick when the ball comes near. Allow the child to slide along the dividing pole rather than move to the left and right with it.

- Encourage children who are unilateral to place both hands on the pole during foosball, positioning the unaffected hand on top of the affected one.

Controlled kick 2

Area: *Games*

Objectives:

❋ to develop stability of the hip and shoulder girdle;

❋ to enhance strength in upper limbs;

❋ to explore new ways of moving in space.

Equipment:

❋ 8 short cones to serve as goalposts;

❋ marking tape or chalk;

❋ 4 large foam balls.

Lesson summary	
Warm-up: Limb lift	10 mins
Crab goal	5–10 mins
Creeping crabs	5–10 mins
Crab attack	5–10 mins
Cool-down	5 mins

Activity	**Purpose**	**Curriculum links:** *England* **/** Scotland

Warm-up: Limb lift
◉ Children carry out the following tasks:
  On all fours, lift right leg, hold position and count to 10. Repeat with left leg.
  On all fours, lift right arm, hold position and count to 10. Repeat with left arm.
  On all fours, lift right arm and left leg, hold position and count to 10. Repeat with opposite arm and leg.
  On all fours, lift right arm and left leg, hold position and count to 5. Repeat with opposite arm and leg.
  In crab position – with tummy facing up and balancing on feet and hands (straight arms) – lift right leg up, hold position and count to 5. Repeat with left leg.
	Developing controlled balance
	Enhancing stability of the hip and shoulder girdle
	
	1a, 1b, 8a
	1a, 1b, 2a	

Crab goal ◉ Create 4 goals using cones positioned 2m apart. Mark a starting line 3m away from each goal. ◉ Children get into 4 teams. Provide each team with a large foam ball. Appoint a runner for each team who will fetch and position the ball. ◉ In turn, each team member balances in crab position, on hands and feet with arms straight and tummy facing up. The runner positions the ball so they can try to kick the ball between the cones – while maintaining the crab position. ◉ The team scoring the most goals in a 5–10 minute period are the winners. ◉ Ensure the runner gets an opportunity to attempt a goal.	Strengthening hip and shoulder girdle *1a, 1b, 2b, 2c, 7a* *1a, 3a, 3b, 4c, 5a, 5b*	

Activity	Purpose	Curriculum links: *England* / Scotland
Creeping crabs ◎ As above, but the ball must be positioned 2m away from the crab – who must crawl to the ball before kicking it.	Strengthening hip and shoulder girdle This activity requires considerable stamina, so allow children to rest when they feel the need.	*1a, 1b, 2b, 2c, 7a, 7b* 1a, 3a, 3b, 4c, 5a, 5b
Crab attack ◎ This activity is similar to Creeping crabs, but two crabs will attempt to reach the ball and score a goal for their team. ◎ Children remain in 4 teams. Pair the teams up to play against each other, and give each team member a number. ◎ Remove two goals so that only two goals and starting lines remain. ◎ When a number is called, the child who has been allocated that number must crab crawl forwards 2m to the kicking line and attempt to kick the ball into the goal. If the goal is missed, no points are awarded. ◎ The team scoring the most goals win. *Variations* Each team member must crab crawl towards the ball and kick it towards a goal. Once kicked the next person sets off. One child can be allocated as ball runner, if necessary. The team that scores the most goals in a given period are the winners.	Extending hip and shoulder stability and strength	*1a, 1b, 2b, 2c, 7a, 7b, 7c* 1a, 2b, 3a, 3b, 5a, 5b
Cool-down ◎ Children lie on the floor in a space and carry out the following tasks: Slowly raise the right leg up straight, hold and count to 5. Repeat with the left leg. Slowly raise the right arm upwards and count to 5. Repeat with the left arm. Attempt to lift both legs up straight, hold and count to 5. Lie flat on the floor, take 5 deep breaths, then stand up.	Stretching and relaxing all limb muscles	*1a, 1b, 2a* 1b, 2a

Recap   *3a, 3b, 3c, 4a, 4b*   1b, 6a

- Discuss which part of the body was most active during this session. Explain that their arms ached because they were holding up the whole of the trunk, and this was made harder with the pull of gravity. Briefly discuss what gravity is.
- Why is it important that our shoulders are strong? (To help us carry things, lift objects onto shelves, swim, etc.) Can you think of any more things we do that need strength in the shoulders?

Additional differentiation

- For a children with limited or restricted mobility, you can modify the crab position by allowing them to leave their bottom on the floor. Then encourage the child to push forwards across the floor with their bottom on the ground, rather than lifting their body weight.
- Children with low muscle tone (as with DCD or Down syndrome) will need frequent rests during the crab activities because shoulder- and hip-girdle stability will be weak. Encourage them to maintain the crab position, but for shorter periods.

Lesson 18

Accurate kick

Area: *Games*

Objectives:
* to develop controlled foot–eye coordination;
* to encourage accurate spatial assessment and organisation;
* to develop accurate foot-strike action.

Equipment:
* beanbags or footballs – 1 each for half the class;
* Brazilian footballs or other small weighted balls – 1 each for half the class;
* footballs – 1 each for half the class;
* Reflex soccer balls or balloons (not fully inflated, with an attached string of approx. 2m) – 1 for each child;
* 4–6 targets (e.g. Spordas Targetwall™) or 4 sheets of card (1.5m x 1.5m) with painted circles;
* 4–6 Velcro® balls (optional);
* marking tape or chalk.

Lesson summary

Warm-up: Coach commands	5 mins
Pass and stop	10 mins
Return kick	5 mins
Penalty kick	10 mins
Penalty run	10 mins
Cool-down	5 mins
Recap	

Activity	Purpose	Curriculum links: *England* / Scotland
Warm-up: Coach commands ◎ Ask the children to imagine that you are the coach for their favourite football team. Instruct them to: jog on the spot; jog on the spot, drawing knees up to chin; run round the room, changing direction on command; move round the room taking 2 hops on one leg then 2 on the other; conclude with 5 star jumps and a loud shout for your favourite team.	Warming up muscles ready to play football	*1a, 1b, 2a, 2b, 2c, 7a* 1a, 1b, 2a, 2b, 3a, 3b
Pass and stop ◎ Children get into pairs. Give each pair a beanbag or football. ◎ Children in each pair stand 2m apart and kick the beanbag to each other, ensuring that it is stopped before it is passed back. Following 3 successful passes, they take a step back. ◎ Continue up to a distance of 5m. ◎ Repeat with a heavy small ball such as a Brazilian football. ◎ Repeat with an ordinary football.	Developing foot–eye coordination	*1a, 1b, 2a, 2b, 2c, 7a* 2a, 2b, 3a, 3b, 5a, 5b

© *Get Physical!* LDA   Permission to Photocopy

Activity	Purpose	Curriculum links: *England* / Scotland

Return kick

◎ Give each child a Reflex soccer ball (or balloon with a length of string attached). They hold the end of the string and practise kicking the ball with each foot.

◎ Practise kicking the ball forwards.

Developing self-regulation of kick with an object which will remain near

1a, 1b, 2a, 2b, 2c, 7a
2a, 3a, 3b

Penalty kick

◎ If commercially produced targets are not available, use large sheets of card (approx. 1.5m) and paint on them 4 or 5 coloured circles of differing sizes (e.g. 50cm, 35cm, 20cm). Allocate 10 points to the smallest circle, 5 to the medium-sized circles and 2 to the largest circle. Prop the targets against a wall. (If a Targetwall™ is used, Velcro® balls can be used to making scoring easier.)

◎ Place a penalty spot 2–3m in front of each target.

◎ Put the children in teams of 4–6. Teams practise kicking a football from the penalty spot against the target to hit the selected circles.

◎ Add a competitive element by playing teams against each other, to see who can score the most points.

Developing accurate strike and foot–eye coordination

1a, 1b, 2a, 2b, 2c, 7a, 7b
2a, 3a, 3b, 5a, 5b

Penalty run

◎ As above, but provide a run-in line marked 2m from the penalty spot.

◎ Players must take it in turn to run to the spot and then kick the ball to the target.

Developing accurate strike and ball skills within the context of a limited environment with restricted spatial planning

1a, 1b, 2a, 2b, 2c, 7a, 7b, 7c
2a, 3a, 3b, 5a, 5b

Cool-down

◎ The whole class forms a circle. Then choose 4 children to take a football each, and create an inner circle.

◎ Children carefully pass the footballs from the inner to the outer circle. Encourage each child to stop the ball before returning it.

Drawing children together to rehearse skills introduced

1a, 1b, 2a, 2b, 2c, 7a
2a, 2b, 3a, 3b, 4c, 5a, 5b

Recap   *3a, 3b, 3c, 4a, 4b*   3a, 6a

- Discuss the importance of stopping a moving object before kicking it back, to aid accuracy. Was it easier to target a heavier object or a lighter one? Why do you think heavier objects were used before footballs?

Lesson 19

Observation and invasion games 1

Area: *Games*

Objectives:

* to encourage the rapid assessment of space needed when playing invasion games;

* to enhance visual figure–ground discrimination;

* to develops group tactics.

Equipment:

* 4–6 hula hoops, each a different colour;

* 36 beanbags of 6 colours to match the hula hoops;

* 20–25 short cones (e.g Super Safe Flexi Cones);

* stopwatch or egg timer;

* whistle (optional);

* 4–6 gym mats.

Lesson summary

Warm-up: Remote control	5 mins
Touch blue	5 mins
Beanbag raid	5–10 mins
Colour-blind, colour-conscious	5–10 mins
Cups and saucers	5–10 mins
Cool-down	5 mins
Recap	

Activity	Purpose	Curriculum links: *England* / Scotland
Warm-up: Remote control ◉ Ask children to imagine that they are video or DVD players, and that you are operating the remote control. They move according to your instructions: 　　play – walk forwards; 　　rewind – walk backwards; 　　pause – stand still; 　　fast forward – run at speed; 　　fast rewind – run backwards; 　　stop – stop; 　　record – a silly dance; 　　flick channels – rapid change of actions selected by you; e.g. stand, sit, turn, roll. ◉ Allow a child to take over the operation of the remote control.	Developing initial concepts of forwards, back, stop, start, up and down	*1a, 1b, 2a, 2b, 2c, 6b* 1a, 1b, 2b, 3a, 3b
Touch blue ◉ Children stand in a space. You call out a command to touch a particular type of object, e.g., 'touch blue', whereupon all the children must select something in the room of that colour and run to touch it. Vary the commands, e.g. they could touch objects of specified: 　　colours; 　　shapes; 　　sizes; 　　textures.	Developing visual and auditory figure–ground discrimination	*1a, 1b, 2a, 2b, 2c, 7a* 3a, 4b, 5a, 5b

　　　© *Get Physical!* LDA　Permission to Photocopy

Activity	Purpose	Curriculum links: *England* / Scotland

Beanbag raid

◎ Put the children into 4 teams, giving each team a colour with a matching hula hoop as a base. Place beanbags in the centre of the room: 6 of each of the 4 colours.

◎ On the word 'Go', each team must run and collect as many beanbags as possible (especially the beanbags of their own team colour) and return them to their base. However, only one beanbag may be carried at a time. Teams may also steal beanbags from other teams' bases.

◎ Points are awarded to each team as follows: 5 points for each beanbag of the team's own colour; 2 points for each beanbag of another colour.

◎ This is a fast game. Teams may wish to think about tactics – e.g. they may decide to have a couple of defenders by their base to prevent beanbags being stolen, swapping roles during the game.

Encouraging rapid assessment of space

1a, 1b, 2a, 2b, 2c, 7a, 7b, 7c
1a, 2b, 3a, 4b, 5a, 5b

Colour-blind, colour-conscious

◎ Put the class into 2 teams (or, if the class is large, 4 teams, but only 2 teams play at any time). Designate one team as 'colour blind' and the other as 'colour-conscious'.

◎ Scatter 4–6 coloured hula hoops across the hall, and place between 24 and 36 coloured beanbags in each hoop. Half the beanbags in the hoop should match the colour of the hoop, and half should be a different colour to match the other hoops.

◎ On the word 'Go', the colour-blind team must remove beanbags from matching hoops and place them in non-matching hoops; those who are in the colour-conscious team simultaneously must try to get the beanbags into hoops of matching colour. Time the race for 3 minutes, then blow a whistle or shout 'Stop'.

◎ This game is fast and furious. The winning team are determined by the number of beanbags either matched or mismatched.

Developing visual figure–ground discrimination

1a, 1b, 2a, 2b, 2c, 7a, 7b
1a, 2b, 3a, 3b, 4b, 5a, 5b

Activity	Purpose	Curriculum links: England / Scotland
Cups and saucers ◎ Take 20–25 small cones and place them randomly around the room, half facing down (saucers) and half facing upwards (cups). ◎ Put the class into two teams: one to be the 'cups', the other the 'saucers'. On the word 'Go', children have to try to turn all the cones into either cups or saucers, depending on their team. Time the race for 3 minutes, then blow a whistle or shout 'Stop'. ◎ The team with the most converted cones are the winners	Developing visual figure–ground discrimination, and appreciation of the concepts 'up' and 'down' This provides an opportunity to observe spatial organisation.	*1a, 1b, 2a, 2b, 2c, 7a 7c* *1a, 2b, 3a, 3b, 4b, 5a, 5b*
Cool-down ◎ Put the class into 4–6 teams, and give each a mat to sit on. All mats are the same distance from where you are standing. ◎ When you call out an item that is in the room, one child in each team must bring it to you as quickly as possible. Teams rotate runners. The first team to get an item to you gets a point.	Less busy, controlled activity involving observation and speed	*1a, 1b, 2a, 2b, 2c, 7a* *1b, 2a, 5a, 5b*

Recap   *3a, 3b, 3c, 4a, 4b*   *2a, 5a, 6a*

- Talk about the fact that today's games were very fast, and children had to make rapid movements and use avoidance strategies to prevent collisions. Think about which sports require such tactics.

- Ask how they decided who was going to be in attack and who in defence for the team games. Why? What skills are needed for each of these roles?

- Emphasise how both attack and defence positions depend on each other. One is not more important than the other, especially in Beanbag raid.

Additional differentiation

- Children with perceptual problems may struggle to accommodate to the speed of movement. They may be helped by being put in the defending position during Beanbag raid or by having only 4 players in each team in order to restrict the number of people moving at any time.

Objectives:

✻ to develop observation skills;

✻ to enhance body awareness and body schema;

✻ to develop controlled movement.

Equipment:

✻ ball;

✻ a bag of multi-coloured clothes pegs (pinch clip variety);

✻ marking tape or chalk;

✻ 4 hula hoops;

✻ whistle (optional);

✻ coloured tags with Velcro® ends (e.g. Rip Tags™) or pieces of coloured ribbon (approx. 25cm long);

✻ stopwatch or egg timer.

Lesson summary

Warm-up: I notice you	5 mins
Where's Peggy?	10 mins
Peg pass	10 mins
Cat's tails	10 mins
Cool-down	5–10 mins
Recap	

Activity	Purpose	Curriculum links: *England* / Scotland
Warm-up: I notice you ◎ Children stand in a circle (or several small circles, depending on class size). ◎ Pass a ball round the circle from child to child. As it is passed, the thrower must make a comment about the person they are passing to – e.g. red shirt, cut on knee. Encourage varied and rapid responses.	Developing an awareness of body image through observation of others	*1a, 1b, 2a, 2b, 2c, 7a* 2a, 5a, 5b, 6a

Where's Peggy?
 	
◎ Put the class into 4–6 teams. Provide each team with 5 pegs. Mark starting and finishing lines.
 	
◎ A child from each team is positioned at the finishing line, as 'Peggy'.
 	
◎ The rest of the team take turns to pick up a peg and cross the room to attach it to the clothes of the awaiting Peggy. Their mode of travel across the room is determined by where the peg is to be placed. Each time, you call out one of the following:
 	
    Peggy's sleeves – travel across room using arms only (commando crawl);
 	
    Peggy's apron – slither on tummy;
 	
    Peggy's back – slide on back;
 	
    Peggy's bloomers – bottom shuffle;
 	
    Peggy's slippers – hop.
 	
◎ Once all pegs have been attached appropriately, the team shout 'Peggy's here!' The first team to place the final peg and shout out are the winners.
	Linking actions to body parts
	
	1a, 1b, 2a, 2b, 2c, 7a
	1a, 3a, 3b, 4a, 4b, 5a

Activity	Purpose	Curriculum links: England / Scotland
Peg pass		
◎ Put the class into teams of 4–6. Provide a coloured hula hoop as a base and place 10 matching coloured pegs inside it.	The game requires dodge and aversion tactics as well as subtle invasion.	
◎ Each team stands by their hoop, and on the word 'Go' they discreetly clip their pegs onto the clothing of opposing team members. If a peg is discovered, it may be removed and placed on someone else's clothing.	Extending observation and body awareness	
◎ After 5 minutes, blow a whistle or shout 'Stop'. Each team returns to their base and the number of pegs attached to their players is counted. The team with the fewest pegs attached are the winners.		
◎ This game requires subtlety rather than speed.		*1a, 1b, 2a, 2b, 2c, 7a, 8a* 1a, 2b, 3a, 3b, 4b, 5a, 5b
Cats' tails		
◎ Children stay in the same teams. Give each child a tag to stick on to their back (or coloured ribbon which is tucked into the back of their waistband) and hang down as a tail. All members of each team have the same colour tail.	The game requires dodge and aversion tactics as well as subtle invasion.	
◎ On the word 'Go', the children must try to capture as many tails as possible.	Developing proprioceptive awareness	
◎ After 5 minutes, blow a whistle or shout 'Stop'. The team who have captured the most tails are the winners.		*1a, 1b, 2a, 2b, 2c, 7a, 7c* 1a, 2b, 3a, 3b, 4b, 5a, 5b
Cool-down		
◎ Children sit on the floor in pairs. One of the pair turns away while the other makes 3 subtle changes in their appearance – e.g. swapping shoes, rolling up a sleeve, tucking hair behind the ear.	Developing acute observation skills, which help with motor control and body awareness	
◎ Their partner must try to spot what has changed. Once they have identified all 3, the pair change positions.		*1a, 1b, 2a, 2b, 2c* 6a

Recap   *3a, 3b, 3c, 4a, 4b*   6a

- Discuss how and why today's activities required careful observation. Talk about why it is important to look carefully at things. Consider how a baby learns. How do we develop our motor skills? How do we learn new skills?

- Did anyone struggle to notice the differences in their partner's appearance? If so, why?

- Observation and attention need effort and concentration. Discuss how these are needed for playing a computer game. How does this differ from watching and listening in class? Which is easier?

Lesson 21 Observation and listening skills

Area: *Gymnastic activities*

You could adopt a royal theme in this lesson.

Objectives:

- to develop listening skills;
- to develop sequential memory;
- to enhance motor skills and coordination.

Equipment:

None required

Lesson summary

Warm-up: Simon says	5 mins
Royal court	5 mins
Royal decrees	5–10 mins
Knights, horses and cavaliers	5–10 mins
On board the royal yacht	10 mins
Cool-down	5 mins
Recap	

Activity	Purpose — Curriculum links: *England* / Scotland
Warm-up: Simon says ◎ Play Simon says, incorporating warm-up exercises such as jumping, stretches, hopping, skipping. ◎ The aim of the game is to listen carefully and follow the appropriate instructions. If you are adopting the royal theme, this game could be played as 'Sir Simon says'.	Encouraging movement to warm-up the muscles while encouraging the children to develop listening skills *1a, 1b, 2a, 2b, 2c, 8b* 1a, 1b, 3a, 4b
Royal court ◎ Children sit in a large circle and are randomly assigned one of the following court characters: jester, juggler, maid, dancer, knight, prince, princess. ◎ When you call out a character, all children with that title must stand up and swap places as quickly as possible.	Developing listening skills and responses *1a, 1b, 2a, 2b, 2c, 8a* 3a, 3b, 5a, 5b
Royal decrees ◎ Children stand in a space. You give a series of sound signals, to which the children must make the agreed response, e.g: clap – star jump; finger click – hop on the right leg; stamp – hop on the left leg; slap thighs – stretch and touch toes. ◎ Encourage children to relate the sounds to the actions without the need for verbal prompts. Restrict the number of sounds and actions when working with Reception and Y1.	Developing auditory discrimination and sequential memory *1a, 1b, 2a, 2b, 2c, 8a, 8b* 2a, 3a, 3b, 4b

Activity	Purpose	Curriculum links: England / Scotland

Knights, horses and cavaliers

◎ Children work in pairs (ideally girl and boy). Pairs walk together around the room; when you call 'knights', 'horses' or 'cavaliers', they must respond accordingly:

> knights – one child lifts the other from the floor in either an arm lift or piggy back;
>
> horses – one child gets down on all fours and the other stands astride their back (as if riding a horse);
>
> cavaliers – one child drops onto one knee and provides a seat with the other knee; the other child sits on the raised knee.

◎ The last pair performing the appropriate action each time are out. The last pair in are the winners.

Developing auditory attention, auditory memory and rapid response to requests

1a, 1b, 2a, 2b, 2c, 8a, 8b
2a, 3a, 3b, 5a, 5b, 6a

On board the royal yacht

◎ Children imagine they are on a ship which is positioned centrally in the room. One side of the room is designated as port; the opposite side is starboard. When 'Port' or 'Starboard' is called, the children must run as fast as possible to the appropriate side. Additional commands can be added as follows:

> Man the decks – central position.
>
> Scrub the deck – lie tummy-down and pretend to be scrubbing the floor.
>
> Climb the mast – pretend to climb up a pole.
>
> Sailor overboard! – balance on one leg and scream for help.
>
> Royal visit – all bow to the floor.

◎ If this game is played competitively, the last child to do the correct action each time is out.

Developing listening skills and response to request without the help of a partner

1a, 1b, 2a, 2b, 2c, 8a, 8b
2b, 3a, 3b, 4b, 5a

Cool-down

◎ Children walk around the room. When you call out either 'King' or 'Queen', they respond accordingly:

> King – stand with feet together and slowly bend to bow.
>
> Queen – stand with one foot behind the other, perform a slow, low curtsey.

Flexing and extending activity

1a, 1b, 2a, 2b, 2c
1b, 2a, 2b

Recap   *3a, 3b, 3c, 4a, 4b*   *6a*

- This lesson emphasises the importance of listening before doing. Discuss how easy or hard this was.
- How did children compensate when they did not listen well enough to follow the instructions? Did they copy each other? Did anyone try to anticipate what was coming next?
- Which activity did children find easiest and why? Which was hardest? Was it hard to listen to instructions when everyone was moving at the same time?
- Link this back to a discussion about concentrating in the classroom, emphasising the importance of listening to the right directions and not relying on copying from others.

Additional differentiation

- For children with cerebral palsy, the fast processing and motor responses required for these games may be difficult. If this is so, alter the rules to emphasise control and response rather than speed – e.g. allocate points for maintaining a position correctly rather than for speed of response.
- If a child uses a powered chair, use this for all activities, but emphasise the need to stretch the upper and lower limbs as much as possible. For example, in On board the royal yacht, adapt movements so that the child can participate from the chair:

    Scrub the deck – reach to toes and demonstrate scrubbing action.
    Climb the mast – stretch arms above head.
    Sailor overboard! – lift one arm and extend leg on same side.
    Royal visit – touch toes.

    Encourage as much independent movement as possible.

Lesson 22 Movement in space 1

Area: *Gymnastic activities*

Objectives:

❋ to develop spatial awareness;

❋ to assess distance and location within a mobile environment;

❋ to develop coordinated movement.

Equipment:

❋ 6–8 coloured hula hoops.

Lesson summary

Warm-up: Clumps	5 mins
Cat and mouse	5 mins
Under and over	5–10 mins
Threading race	5–10 mins
Story ladder	5–10 mins
Cool-down	5 mins
Recap	

Activity	Purpose	Curriculum links: England / Scotland
Warm-up: Clumps ◎ Children move around the room in the direction or manner you call, i.e. forwards, backwards, sideways, slowly, fast. ◎ You call 'Stop', followed by a random number less than the class size. Children must stop and as quickly as possible form a clump with the corresponding number of members. Any remainders are out – until the next game begins. *Variation* Add a position such as 'back to back'.	Encouraging observation of space within a mobile environment Developing listening skills and collaborative teamwork	*1a, 1b, 2a, 2b, 2c, 8a* *1a, 2b, 3a, 5a*
Cat and mouse ◎ Children sit in a circle. Select a child to be the cat, who prowls round outside the circle. Select a mouse from the circle by subtly touching a child on the shoulder. ◎ The mouse must run around the circle and get back to their place while the cat gives chase. Both must travel in the same direction. ◎ If the mouse is caught, the cat has another opportunity to play. If the mouse is not caught, they return to their place. ◎ Change the cat and mouse.	Developing anticipatory action	*1a, 1b, 2a, 2b, 2c, 8a, 8b* *3a, 3b, 4b, 5a, 5b*
Under and over ◎ Put the class into teams of approx. 6–8. Each team stands in a line, and the child at the front has a hula hoop. ◎ On the word 'Go', the first child puts the hoop over their head, steps through and passes it to the next team member, who does the same. The first team to get their hoop to the back are the winners. ◎ Race again, but this time the hoop goes over the head of the first child, who steps through and passes it to the next team member, who steps in and draws the hoop upwards. In this way, the hoop passes alternately upwards and downwards along the whole team.	Developing coordinated whole-body movement, team cooperation and spatial planning Encouraging personal organisation skills	*1a, 1b, 2a, 2b, 2c, 8a, 8b* *2a, 3a, 3b, 4b, 5a, 5b*

Activity	**Purpose**	**Curriculum links:** *England* / Scotland

Threading race

◎ Children stay in the same teams and keep the same hoops. The first child in the team must hold the hoop vertically, with the bottom edge approx. 50cm from the ground.

◎ The rest of the team hold hands, and when the race is started each member must climb through the hoop as if crawling through a tunnel. Once all the team are through, the hoop is passed to the second person and the process is repeated until all the team have had the opportunity to hold the hoop.

Developing coordination and spatial planning

1a, 1b, 2a, 2b, 2c, 8a, 8b
2a, 3a, 3b, 5a, 5b

Story ladder

◎ Put the class into two teams. Within each team, the children get into pairs and sit on the floor facing each other, with their legs straight and soles of the feet touching. The pairs are arranged in a line, with a small space of 0.5m between the pairs – to create a ladder formation.

◎ Choose a story – e.g. Noah's ark – and name each pair according to a character in the story – e.g. Mr Noah, Mrs Noah, elephants, camels.

◎ Tell the story, and when a character is mentioned, the corresponding pair must stand up, step down the ladder, run around the edges and return down the ladder to their places without standing on anyone.

◎ If they are playing competitively, someone can keep score, giving a point to the fastest team each time.

Developing spatial planning, concentration and listening skills

1a, 1b, 2a, 2b, 2c, 8a, 8b, 8c
3a, 3b, 4c, 5a, 5b

Activity	Purpose	Curriculum links: *England* / Scotland
Cool-down ◎ Lead the class in singing 'Old MacDonald had a farm' but instead of naming animals, suggest an action such as 2 jumps, 1 clap, 3 stamps or 1 turn. For example, 'Old MacDonald had a farm, E, i, e, i, o. And on that farm he gave a stomp. E, i, e, i, o.' ◎ Encourage the class to remember the actions in the correct order.	Requiring good attention and rapid responses Drawing whole group together again	*1a, 1b, 2a, 2b, 2c, 8a, 8b* 3a, 3b, 5a

Recap   *3a, 3b, 3c, 4a, 4b*   2a, 2b, 5a, 5b, 6a

• Discuss how hard it is to control fast movements in a restricted space, as in Clumps and Story ladder. What tactics did the children use to stop themselves from bumping into each other or from stepping on others? For example, did they slow movements down, or change body position? Relate this to school rules such as not running indoors and not rushing around in the classroom.

• Discuss the final balancing games and the skills needed to succeed at this: teamwork, good listening skills, help from others and balance.

Additional differentiation

• In Story ladders, allow any child who is dependent on a wheelchair to complete a full rotation of the group, rather than moving along the ladder.

Objectives:

✳ to encourage spatial perception during movement;

✳ to develop spatial awareness with simultaneous observation skills;

✳ to develop balance and body awareness.

Equipment:

✳ coloured mats (e.g. Spordas Space Stations™), carpet squares, or named A4 cards – 1 for each child;

✳ red, yellow and green cards – 1 of each colour;

✳ beanbags – 1 for each child;

✳ CD player and music (optional).

Lesson summary

Warm-up: Home and away	5 mins
Avoid and run	5 mins
Traffic lights	5 mins
Fruit salad	5–10 mins
Scarecrow tag	5 mins
Frozen beanbag	5–10 mins
Cool-down	5 mins
Recap	

Activity	Purpose Curriculum links: *England / Scotland*
Warm-up: Home and away ◉ Provide a coloured mat (or carpet square or A4 card) for each child. Children run around the room in a variety of directions as you instruct – e.g. forwards, backwards, sideways. When you call 'Stop', they return to their own places. The main point of the activity is to run round and return to places without bumping into anyone.	Developing an awareness of space and distance in respect to an object and to each other *1a, 1b, 2b, 2c, 8a* *1a, 2a, 2b, 5a*
Avoid and run ◉ Children run around the room in various directions as you instruct – e.g. forwards, backwards, sideways, slowly, jerkily, fast – again, trying not to bump into anyone. If children collide, the child who caused the collision must sit out.	A precursor to Traffic lights, which serves to help children increase speed and direction of movement without colliding with each other *1a, 2b, 8a* *1a, 2a, 2b, 3b*

Traffic lights
 	
◉ Children run round the room in a direction you have instructed. When you hold up a coloured card, everyone reacts accordingly:
 	
    red – stop;
 	
    yellow – slow to a walking pace;
 	
    green – move quickly around the room.
 	
◉ Children need to control their movement while observing the card signals. Any child who fails to respond to the traffic lights is 'pulled up by the police' and sits out. Anyone crashing must also sit out.
	Encouraging movement at speed along with observation skills
	
	Children will succeed only if they observe the cards. This will also reveal which children are dependent upon verbal prompts to control their movements.
	
	1a, 1b, 2b, 2c, 8a
	1a, 2b, 3a, 3b, 4b

Activity	Purpose	Curriculum links: *England / Scotland*

Fruit salad

◎ Children sit in a circle on the floor. Each child chooses an item of fruit and declares their choice to the group.

◎ When you call out the name of a fruit, all children who have chosen that fruit must stand up and swap places as quickly as possible without collision.

◎ The last person standing is either out, or selects the next fruit.

Developing observation, spatial planning, motor planning and organisation

1a, 1b, 2b, 2c, 8a
2a, 2b, 5a, 5b

Scarecrow tag

◎ Choose a child to be the farmer; the rest are scarecrows who have escaped from the field. The farmer must try to catch the scarecrows who, when tagged, stand still with their legs astride and arms horizontal. They are released if another scarecrow crawls through their legs.

◎ The farmer may enlist neighbouring farmers from amongst the class members playing scarecrows to help round up the remaining scarecrows.

Spatial planning involving varying levels

Rather than focusing on one level, this activity demands controlled spatial planning in crouching, squatting and crawling.

1a, 1b, 2b, 2c, 8a, 8b
1a, 2a, 2b, 3a, 3b, 5a, 5b

Frozen beanbag

◎ Give each child a beanbag, which they balance on their head. They may not use hands to help keep it on.

◎ The children move around as you direct – e.g. forwards, backwards, with a wide stride, on tiptoes. Alternatively they could move to music. If the beanbag falls off, the child is frozen and must stand completely still. They may be rescued by someone bending down (while keeping their own beanbag in position) and replacing the fallen beanbag.

◎ The winner is the person who has helped the most people to 'defrost'.

Controlled movement and spatial planning which incorporates balance and postural control

1a, 1b, 2b, 2c, 8a, 8b
2a, 2b, 3a, 3b, 6a

Activity	Purpose	Curriculum links: *England* / Scotland
Cool-down ◎ Each child balances the beanbag on their head, as in the preceding game. They walk round the room very slowly, maintaining the balanced position and carefully avoiding any collisions. ◎ Once they have made a full circuit of the room, they should try to sit down slowly, keeping the beanbag in place.	Calming activity requiring balance and postural control.	*1a, 1b, 2b, 2c, 8a* 1b, 2a, 2b

Recap   *3a, 3b, 3c, 4a, 4b*   2a, 2b, 3a, 3b, 6a

- Discuss whether the children found the activities progressively more difficult, as each activity required more control. Frozen beanbag, especially, demands good balance skills. Identify the winner of this game, stressing the slightly unusual emphasis: not to be the fastest, but to help others.

- Discuss how this can be applied outside the classroom. How does it feel when you help someone else?

Additional differentiation

- Children who have restricted mobility can undertake all activities in a wheelchair. In Scarecrow tag, the child may extend their arms or legs to allow others to crawl under.

Objectives:

✳ to develop hip and shoulder stability;

✳ to develop increased stamina while balancing;

✳ to develop reciprocal movements.

Equipment:

✳ marking tape or chalk;

✳ plastic hand and foot shapes (e.g. Throw Down Hands and Feet), or card foot and hand shapes which can be drawn and cut out in class (with sticky tack to secure);

✳ plastic mini-beasts (optional);

✳ stopwatch (optional).

Lesson summary

Warm-up: Creature walks	5 mins
Elephant walk	5 mins
Creature races	5 mins
Explorer's trail	5 mins
Mini-beast escape	10 mins
Our trail	5 mins
Mini-beast race	5 mins
Cool-down	5 mins
Recap	

Activity	Purpose	Curriculum links: *England / Scotland*
Warm-up: Creature walks ◎ Children crawl around the room like: 　　a tortoise (slowly); 　　a leopard (slinkily); 　　a spider (sideways). They make one circuit of the room for each creature.	Developing controlled shoulder- and hip-girdle stability	*1a, 1b, 2a, 2b, 2c, 8a, 8b* 1a, 2a, 2b, 4a
Elephant walk ◎ The children try to walk once round the room with their hands on the floor and legs straight.	Requiring controlled balance and reciprocal arm and leg movements	*1a, 1b, 2a, 2b, 2c, 8a, 8b* 2a, 2b, 3a
Creature races ◎ Mark a starting line at one side of the room and a parallel finishing line 12m away. Put children in 4 or 5 teams. ◎ The first child in each team must cross the room, crawling on all fours like a leopard. When they have crossed the finishing line, the next child sets off, moving in the same way. The winning team are the first with everyone across the finishing line. ◎ Have 2 further races with teams moving like spiders (sideways) and elephants (stooped with hands on floor and legs straight).	Requiring reciprocal crawling motion	*1a, 1b, 2a, 2b, 2c, 8a, 8b* 1a, 2b, 3a, 3b, 4b, 5a
Explorer's trail ◎ Place the hand shapes on the floor. In small groups, the children attempt to crawl across the floor placing their hands on the outlines. ◎ Plastic mini-beasts could be placed strategically around the room to add interest.	Encouraging balance using both upper and lower limbs	*1a, 1b, 2a, 2b, 2c, 8a, 8c, 8d* 3a, 4b, 5a, 6a

Activity	Purpose	Curriculum links: *England* / Scotland

Mini-beast escape

◎ Put the children into 4 groups.

◎ Each group creates a trail across the room using hand and foot shapes.

◎ Children take turns to cross each trail by placing their hands on hand shapes and their feet on foot shapes.

Encouraging balance using both upper and lower limbs

◎ On completing a trail, the group progresses onto the next trail and so on until all the trails have been completed.

1a, 1b, 2a, 2b, 2c, 8a, 8b
3a, 3b, 4b, 5a, 5b

Our trail

◎ Put the class into small groups. Each group must collaborate to create their own trail, placing pictures of feet and hands appropriately on the floor. The group must be able to follow their own trail.

Group cooperation

1a, 1b, 2a, 2b, 2c, 8a, 8d
3a, 3b, 4b, 4c, 5a, 5b

Mini-beast race

◎ Each group has to follow another group's trail as fast as possible. This can be timed, or groups can vie with each other.

Increasing the speed of placement of hands and feet

Maintaining hip and shoulder stability at speed

1a, 1b, 2a, 2b, 2c, 8a, 8b
1a, 2a, 2b, 3a, 3b, 5a, 5b

Cool-down

◎ Children sit in a space on the floor. They draw their knees up to their chin and hold for a count of 5. Then they stretch their legs forwards to the front and count to 5.

◎ Repeat 3 times.

Flexing and extending knees, which have been put under some strain during today's lesson

1a, 1b, 2a, 2b, 2c
1b, 2a, 3b

Recap   *3a, 3b, 3c, 4a, 4b*   2a, 3a, 3b, 6a

• Why is it important that we are able to crawl? Explain that it helps to develop stable shoulders, and that helps us with fine motor tasks such as handwriting.

• How did you decide on the type of trail you created? For example, did you want the other teams to stretch their legs? Did you make it difficult to balance? Did you have to amend this after trying it yourself?

Lesson 25 — Balance on alternate legs 1

Area: *Gymnastic activities*

Objectives:

✳ to balance on either leg;

✳ to develop static and dynamic balance;

✳ to appreciate why this skill is necessary.

Equipment:

✳ a drum or tambourine;

✳ carpet squares (optional) – 1 for each child;

✳ 4 long ropes, or a series of short ropes, or chalk to draw lines on the floor;

✳ stopwatch.

Lesson summary

Warm-up: Funny walks	5 mins
Storks	2 mins
Railway-track waddle walk	5 mins
Group railway-track waddle	10 mins
Push-me pull-you train track walk	10 mins
Cool-down	5 mins
Recap	

Activity	Purpose Curriculum links: *England* / Scotland

Warm-up: Funny walks
 ◎ Children walk twice round the room like:
      a penguin – with very narrow steps;
      a dinosaur – with very wide steps;
      a giraffe – with very long strides.
 ◎ Encourage movement to the rhythm of the drum or tambourine.
	Developing controlled movement
	
	 1a, 1b, 2a, 2b, 2c, 8a
	 1a, 2a, 2b, 4a

Storks ◎ Children balance on their left leg, attempting 20 seconds. Encourage them to set their own targets and to assess their own balance by counting slowly. ◎ Repeat, standing on the right leg. ◎ Very young children could stand on their own carpet square to help control their balance.	Self-monitoring Use this as a guide to personal improvement. *1a, 1b, 2a, 2b, 2c, 8b* 2a, 3b, 6a
Railway-track waddle walk ◎ Place the ropes parallel to each other on the floor about 10cm apart, like a railway track. (Or draw lines using chalk.) In pairs, one child stands behind the other, holding onto their waist. Children move along the tracks with their legs either side of the rope; this will involve rocking from side to side. They should attempt to do this in synchrony. ◎ Each pair goes twice along the track. They start off slowly, gradually increasing speed. ◎ Increase the distance between the ropes by 10cm and repeat. Continue up to a distance of approx. 50cm. ◎ Try altering the speed of movement along the track; slower speed will require more controlled balance on either leg.	Encouraging rocking motion from side to side Demonstrating the transfer of weight required to balance on one leg *1a, 1b, 2a, 2b, 2c, 8a, 8b* 3a, 3b, 4a, 4b

Activity	Purpose	Curriculum links: *England* / Scotland
Group railway-track waddle ◎ Form trains of 4 or 5 children. Children should be positioned behind each other, all facing the same direction and each holding onto the waist of the person in front. Trains move along the track using a rocking motion, in which the entire group rocks simultaneously from right leg to left leg, and so on, gradually moving forward. ◎ Each train travels twice along the track. Alter the speed of the train by calling out 'Slow' or 'Fast'. The slower the speed, the more balance is required. ◎ Introduce an element of competition by timing each group.		*1a, 1b, 2a, 2b, 2c, 8b* 2a, 3a, 3b, 5a, 5b
Push-me pull-you train track walk ◎ Children get into pairs. Children in each pair face each other and hold each other's waists as they move down the track. ◎ Each pair goes twice along the track. If one of the pair is more able, they should move backwards.		*1a, 1b, 2a, 2b, 2c, 8b, 8c* 2b, 3a, 3b, 4b, 5a, 5b
Cool-down Draw everyone back to a central circle, holding hands. Together: raise the right leg forwards and together count slowly to 5; raise the left leg forwards and together count slowly to 5; raise the right leg backwards and together count slowly to 5; raise the left leg backwards and together count slowly to 5; take 5 deep breaths, then rest.	Stretching and balancing	*1a, 1b, 2a, 2b, 2c* 1b, 2a, 5a

Recap   *3a, 3b, 3c, 4a, 4b*   2a, 3a, 6a

- Consider how much control was required during the activities. Was it harder to balance when the ropes were positioned close to each other or further apart? Why is it important to be able to balance on either leg?

Additional differentiation

- For children with restricted mobility, allow funny manoeuvres in the wheelchair rather than funny walks.

- In the railway-track activities, support the child in standing and attempting to manoeuvre along part of the track.

Balance on alternate legs 2

Area: *Gymnastic activities*

Objectives:

- to reinforce skills introduced in previous lesson;
- to extend ability to balance on alternate legs;
- to improve balance and motion skills.

Equipment:

- drum, or tambourine or maracas;
- 20 hula hoops;
- plastic foot shapes (e.g. Throw Down Feet) or card foot shapes which can be drawn and cut out in class (with sticky tack to secure) – at least 40 pairs.

Lesson summary

Warm-up: Waddle run	5 mins
Hoop hop	10 mins
Footstep trail	10 mins
Footstep trail challenge	10 mins
Cool-down	5 mins
Recap	

Activity	Purpose — Curriculum links: *England* / Scotland
Warm-up: Waddle run ◎ Children run round the room with legs as wide as possible, rocking from side to side. ◎ Use the drum (or tambourine or maracas) to create a rhythm. This should alternate between slow and fast.	Developing a sense of rhythm *1a, 1b, 2b, 8a* 1a, 2a, 2b, 4a
Hoop hop ◎ Place a trail of 20 hula hoops on the floor, touching each other to make a zig-zag trail. ◎ Children queue up behind each other at one side of the room. They take turns to travel across the room, placing a foot in each hoop. ◎ Repeat, increasing the speed. ◎ Repeat, providing an element of competition by dividing the class into 4 teams. Each team is timed following the trail. The team completing the hoop trail in the shortest time are the winners.	Requiring balance on each foot *1a, 1b, 2a, 2b, 2c, 8a, 8b* 2a, 2b, 3a, 3b, 5a
Footstep trail ◎ Place the foot shapes randomly on the floor. Children must try to cross the room by placing the right foot on the right-foot shapes, and the left foot on the left-foot shapes. 	Requiring more accurate placement of feet *1a, 1b, 2a, 2b, 2c, 8a, 8b* 2a, 2b, 3a, 3b, 4b

Activity	Purpose	Curriculum links:
		England / Scotland
Footstep trail challenge	Controlled movement and balance, at speed	
◎ Put the class into 4–6 groups. Divide the pairs of foot shapes between the teams.		
◎ Each group creates a trail using foot shapes.		
◎ Each group attempts to follow the other trails, by placing each foot appropriately on the shapes. All trails should be completed by each team.	*1a, 1b, 2a, 2b, 2c, 8a, 8d* 2a, 2b, 3a, 4a, 4b, 5a	
Cool-down	Calming activity incorporating today's movements	
◎ Children walk around the room:		
with a wide gait;		
with a narrow gait;	*1a, 1b, 2a, 2b, 2c* 1b, 2a, 3b	
with either gait, changing direction.		

Recap   *3a, 3b, 3c, 4a, 4b*   3b, 6a

- Was it harder to place your feet on the footprint or in the hoops? Why? Did it become harder when you were competing against each other?

Additional differentiation

- Children who have restricted mobility can either follow activities in supported standing, or negotiate around the hoops and feet in a wheelchair rather than stepping on them.

Objectives:

✳ to develop unilateral balance skills;

✳ to develop motor organisation and planning;

✳ to enhance spatial awareness.

Equipment:

✳ drum (optional);

✳ 20 hula hoops;

✳ stopwatch (optional);

✳ marking tape or chalk;

✳ 4 large paper or plastic plates;

✳ 2 x 20cm batons made of a rolled-up tabloid-sized newspaper (4 batons if class is large).

Lesson summary

Warm-up: Centipede	5 mins
Alternate hoop hop	5 mins
Hoop hopscotch	5 mins
Waiters	10 mins
Jousting	10 mins
Cool-down	5 mins
Recap	

Activity	Purpose	Curriculum links: *England* / Scotland
Warm-up: Centipede ◎ Children make a centipede – a long line with each child holding onto the waist of the person in front. (If the class is large, divide into two groups.) ◎ The centipede moves around the room rocking from side to side, which will require alternately balancing on one leg, then the other. Tell the centipede what speed to move by beating out a rhythm using a drum or a hand clap. Children rock onto the other leg with each beat.	Balancing on one leg for differing periods of time, but with support	*1a, 1b, 2a, 2b, 2c, 6a* 1a, 2a, 3a, 3b, 5a
Alternate hoop hop ◎ Lay 20 hula hoops across the room in a zig-zag pattern, with approx. 10cm between the hoops. ◎ Children must try to cross the room as fast as possible, placing only one foot in each hoop. ◎ After a practice run, the class can be put into 4 teams, and each team can be timed as they cross.	Developing motor planning and organisation	*1a, 1b, 2a, 2b, 2c, 8a, 8b* 2b, 3a, 4b, 5a
Hoop hopscotch ◎ Rearrange the hoops so that they are in a hopscotch format (a single hoop followed by a pair of hoops). ◎ Remaining in 4 teams, children cross the room by hopping in the single hoop and jumping with each foot inside one of the pair of hoops. ◎ When all children have practised the hopscotch movement, have a timed team race.	Developing and maintaining a reciprocal hop and jump action	*1a, 1b, 2a, 2b, 2c, 8a, 8b, 8c* 2b, 3a, 5a

Activity	Purpose	Curriculum links: *England* **/** Scotland
Waiters ◎ Mark a starting line and a parallel finishing line 10m apart. ◎ Children remain in 4 teams and all teams stand behind the starting line. Give the first child in each team a large paper or plastic plate. ◎ That child must hold the plate in the palm of one hand and attempt to hop across the room without its falling off. On reaching the finishing line they must run back and give the plate to the next player in their team. This continues until all players have crossed the room. ◎ If the plate falls off, the child picks it up, replaces it and continues with the race rather than going back to the beginning. ◎ Care rather than speed is essential to the success of this game.	Developing controlled hopping skills	*1a, 1b, 2a, 2b, 2c, 8a* 2a, 3a, 3b, 5a
Jousting ◎ Put the children into two teams (or 4 if the class is large), who sit against the wall opposite each other. Number the children so each child has a corresponding number in the opposite team. ◎ In the centre of the room, place 2 rolled-up pieces of newspaper to serve as batons, and 2 large paper or plastic plates. ◎ When you call out a number, those two children must run to the centre of the room, grab a baton in one hand and balance the plate on the flat palm of their other hand. They must each attempt to knock the plate off their opponent's hand using their baton – while hopping. If they put the other foot down they are not disqualified, but they must be standing on one leg at the moment when their opponent's plate is knocked off. The victor's team gets a point. ◎ Ensure all children have a turn. 	Developing balance and coordination	*1a, 1b, 2a, 2b, 2c, 8a* 2a, 3a, 3b, 5a, 5b
Cool-down ◎ Sitting on the floor, children: 　　raise the right leg upwards and hold for the count of 5; 　　raise the left leg upwards and hold for the count of 5; 　　attempt to raise both legs upwards and hold for the count of 5; 　　shake both legs; 　　relax.	Stretching and relaxing lower limbs	*1a, 1b, 2a, 2b, 2c, 8a* 1b, 2a

Recap *3a, 3b, 3c, 4a, 4b*   2a, 3a, 5b, 6a

- Discuss how difficult it is not only to balance on one leg but also to use your hands at the same time.

- Explain that it is important to slow down an action to develop more control rather than to do things at speed. Refer to the action of carrying a full tray or bucket of water, and point out how important it is to look closely at the object and travel slowly and carefully.

- We tend to think that to be good at PE you have to be fast, but this is not always true. There are certain sports and activities in which movements need to be slowed down in order to be successful, such as gymnastics, bowling and diving. Can the children think of any more?

- This is also true of some activities in the classroom in which speed may affect work; e.g. using scissors, model making and science experiments. Can the children think of tasks that need to be done slowly and carefully?

Additional differentiation

- Children who are dependent upon additional devices to aid their mobility can attempt all tasks with hip support or using a walking aid, although balancing on each leg, rather than hopping, should be encouraged.

- Jousting should be attempted with both feet on the floor and hips supported so that the child can concentrate on upper-limb coordination.

- Children with coordination difficulties such as dyspraxia will struggle to maintain balance on one leg and to hop. Provide a handhold to help the child balance in Waiters and Jousting.

One-leg balance with resistance

Area: *Gymnastic activities*

Objectives:

✱ to maintain balance against resistance;

✱ to develop both static and dynamic balance;

✱ to extend proprioception and kinaesthetic sense.

Equipment:

✱ chalk;

✱ flexible hoops (e.g. large-sized Polymat EverHoops) or skipping ropes – approx. 6.

Lesson summary

Warm-up: Wobbly walks	5 mins
Sumo circle	5 mins
Sumo circle hop	5 mins
Perturbation heckle	5–10 mins
Hop o' war	5–10 mins
Cool-down	5 mins
Recap	

Activity	Purpose	Curriculum links: *England* / Scotland
Warm-up: Wobbly walks ◎ Children walk once round the room in each of the following ways: toe-tug walk – with legs straight, reach down and hold onto toes; heel walk – walk on the heels of the feet only; tiptoe walk – walk on tiptoes, not letting the heels touch the floor; heel–toe walk (forwards) – place the heel of one foot to the toe of the other; heel–toe walk (backwards) – as above, but carefully backwards.	Warming up muscles These activities stretch lower calf muscles ready for balance tasks.	*1a, 1b, 2a, 2b, 2c, 8a* 1a, 1b, 2a, 2b, 3a
Sumo circle ◎ Put the class into 4 groups of 6 or 7 children. Number the groups 1, 2, 3 and 4. Draw two chalk circles on the floor, each approx 2.5m in diameter. ◎ Choose a child from each of groups 1 and 2 to start by standing together inside one circle, and a child from each of groups 3 and 4 to stand in the other. The rest of the group stand outside the circles and act as judges. ◎ The children inside the circle must try to push each other out using their body weight only. Children are disqualified if they shove. ◎ Each team gets 1 point if any of their players manages to push a child outside the circle.	Applying deep pressure through the muscles, thus enhancing kinaesthetic sense	*1a, 1b, 2a, 2b, 2c, 8a, 8b* 3a, 4b, 5a, 6a
Sumo circle hop ◎ As above, but balancing on one leg.	Increasing kinaesthetic sense and balance	*1a, 1b, 2a, 2b, 2c, 8a, 8b* 2a, 3a, 4b, 5a, 6a

Activity	Purpose	Curriculum links: *England /* Scotland
Perturbation heckle		
◎ Create 4 groups of 6 or 7 children.	Providing opportunity to assess attention, concentration, and the child's ability to control motor skills despite being disturbed and disrupted	
◎ One child stands in the middle of the group and balances on one leg. The rest of the group must try to distract the child by heckling and gently touching them as if to knock them over. (No shoving allowed.)		
◎ One member of the group should count slowly to see how long the child is able to maintain one-legged balance under pressure.		
◎ The player who is able to remain balanced on one leg for the longest time can be declared the team champion.		*1a, 1b, 2a, 2b, 2c, 8a, 8b* 2a, 5a
Hop o' war		
◎ Put the class into groups of 4–6, and provide each group with a flexible hoop or skipping rope.	Encouraging balance while increasing proprioceptive skills and kinaesthetic acuity	
◎ For each group, make a mark on the floor in the middle of the room, creating a central point. Put a mark 2m from either side of the central point.		
◎ One child holds each side of the hoop or rope and tries to pull their partner over the line – whilst balancing on one leg. The remaining group members judge the fairness and timing of each competition.		
◎ Ensure that everyone has a go. This should result in each group having a champion to go forward to a class final.		*1a, 1b, 2a, 2b, 2c, 8a, 8b* 1a, 2a, 5a, 5b
Cool-down		
◎ Children find a space, close their eyes and try to balance on one leg.	Self-regulating activity	
◎ They silently count to see how long they can balance without putting their foot down.		
◎ Change legs and repeat.		
◎ Discuss what happened.		*1a, 1b, 2a, 2b, 2c, 8a, 8b* 2a, 5b, 6a

Recap   *3a, 3b, 3c, 4a, 4b*   2a, 3a, 6a

- Today's session required each child to balance against resistance. Discuss the purpose of this in relation to walking on uneven surfaces, and maintaining balance despite being jostled. These situations may occur when, e.g., you are walking on a rough hillside or have to walk along an awkwardly sloping street.

- It is also important to learn to stay upright against resistance to master skills such as riding a bicycle. Ask children to explain what you need to do to ride a bike, emphasising the balance required to go around corners and stay upright on uneven surfaces.

- Can children think of other activities which require similar skills? (e.g. using a scooter, balancing on stilts, using a pogo stick, skateboarding or roller-blading.)

Additional differentiation

- If a child has restricted mobility, allow them to work from the floor, adapting warm-up activities according to individual ability. Sumo circle can be undertaken in a sitting position on the floor, with both children trying to push the other out of the circle from a floor-based position. Sumo circle hop can be carried out from the wheelchair, with the child using upper limbs to resist their partner's pressure to move out of the circle.

- Children who have hemiplegia or hemiparesis should be allowed to balance on 2 legs during Sumo circle hop, Perturbation heckle and Hop o' war.

Upper-limb coordination 1

Area: *Gymnastic activities*

Objectives:

✳ to develop shoulder-girdle stability;

✳ to increase strength in shoulder girdle;

✳ to enhance upper-limb proprioception.

Equipment:

✳ short cones.

Lesson summary

Warm-up: Shoulder shimmy	2 mins
Warm-up: Shoulder-girdle spirals	2 mins
Warm-up: Half press-ups	2 mins
Commando crawl	5 mins
Commando attack	5–10 mins
Commando obstacle course	5–10 mins
Cool-down	5 mins
Recap	

Activity	Purpose	Curriculum links: *England* / Scotland
Warm-up: Shoulder shimmy ◎ Children do a shoulder shimmy consisting of 5 shoulder shrugs forwards, 5 backwards, 5 up, 5 down, and then 5 rotations. ◎ Repeat the shoulder shimmy 5 times.	Warming up the muscles surrounding the shoulder girdle	1a, 1b, 2a, 2b, 2c, 8a 1a, 1b, 2a, 3b
Warm-up: Shoulder-girdle spirals ◎ Children stretch their arms out to the sides in a horizontal position. ◎ They start by making small circles with both arms in one direction, then enlarge these so they become bigger and bigger. When the circles are at maximum size, they alter direction and reduce size. ◎ Attempt 8 spirals (shoulders will tire); 4 in each direction.	Developing strength in shoulder girdle	1a, 1b, 2a, 2b, 2c 1a, 1b, 2a
Warm-up: Half press-ups ◎ Children lie face down on the floor. They try to lift up their tummy by pushing through the arms until they are straight. ◎ This is similar to push-ups, but the tummy can be lifted after the arms are fully stretched. Attempt 5 press-ups.	Weight bearing on upper limbs	1a, 1b, 2a, 2b, 2c 2a, 6a
Commando crawl ◎ Children creep across the room on tummies, using elbows to propel the body. Cross the room 3 or 4 times.	Increasing stamina of upper limbs	1a, 1b, 2a, 2b, 2c, 8a, 8b 1a, 2b, 3a, 5a

Activity	Purpose	Curriculum links: *England* / Scotland
Commando attack ◉ Choose a child to be the look-out. They start turned away, with their back to the rest of the class. ◉ The rest of the class commando-creep across the floor very carefully and quietly. Periodically, the look-out turns, and commandos must stop completely still. Those found moving are out and sit to one side. Commandos must attempt to cross the room without being spotted moving. ◉ Allow 3 or 4 children the opportunity to be a look-out.	Controlled creeping with effort originating in reciprocal creeping motion	*1a, 1b, 2a, 2b, 2c, 8a, 8b* 1a, 2a, 2b, 3a, 5a, 5b
Commando obstacle course ◉ Place a line of small cones across the room. Children commando-creep across the room, meandering in and out of the cones. ◉ If time allows, have timed team races across the room.	Controlled crawling action requiring considerable upper-limb strength *1a, 1b, 2a, 2b, 2c, 8a, 8b, 8c* 1a, 2a, 3a, 5a	
Cool-down ◉ Each child invents a short sequence of movements which incorporates a stretch, curl, roll and twist. They practise this sequence very slowly. ◉ Randomly select children to demonstrate their cool-down sequence to the rest of the class.	Calming activity. *1a, 1b, 2a* 3b, 4a, 5b	

Recap   *3a, 3b, 3c, 4a, 4b*   1b, 5b, 6a

- Discuss which part of the body was making the most effort during today's activities.
- Ask the children to think of tasks requiring them to stretch their arms forwards, e.g. writing on a board, putting books on a shelf, climbing up ladders and ropes.
- When might they need to hold their arms out to the side? Possible examples include holding buckets of water while at the seaside, and carrying heavy bags.
- Discuss which activities made them tire the most quickly. Set a challenge to practise the selected activity.

Lesson 30 — Upper-limb coordination 2

Area: *Gymnastic activities*

Objectives:
✻ to develop strength in the shoulder girdle;

✻ to encourage weight bearing through the shoulders;

✻ to provide proprioceptive feedback through extended arms.

Equipment:
None required.

Lesson summary
Warm-up: Animal walks	5 mins
Bunny hop race	5 mins
Wheelbarrows	5–10 mins
Tipping wheelbarrows	5–10 mins
Cool-down	5 mins
Recap	

Activity	Purpose	Curriculum links: *England / Scotland*

Warm-up: Animal walks
◎ Children move once or twice around the room in each of the following ways:
  giraffe walk – big strides;
  elephant walk – hands on the floor and straight legs;
  tiger prowl – crawling slowly on knees;
  slithery snake – use arms only to slide across floor (commando crawl).
	Increasing awareness of reciprocal hip and shoulder movements	*1a, 1b, 2a, 2b, 2c, 8a, 8b*
		1a, 2a, 2b, 3a, 3b, 4b

Bunny hop race ◎ Children try to bunny hop around the room, putting both hands on the floor, then jumping their feet towards their hands. ◎ Put the children into small teams. Team members bunny hop in turn across the room, then run back to the team.	Developing coordinated movements, applying equal pressure to movements at shoulder and hip Increasing controlled coordination of reciprocal movements.	*1a, 1b, 2a, 2b, 2c, 8b, 8c* *1a, 2a, 2b, 3a, 3b, 5a*
Wheelbarrows ◎ Children get into pairs, and get into wheelbarrow position – one child holds the other round the thighs; the other balances, taking their weight through the hands. ◎ They try to walk forwards a distance of 5–10 metres.	Applying pressure through shoulder girdle	*1a, 1b, 2a, 2b, 2c, 8a, 8b* *2a, 3a, 5a*
Tipping wheelbarrows ◎ In the same pairs, the child being the wheelbarrow tucks in their head and slowly rolls forwards to perform a forward roll.	Increasing stability and stamina of shoulder girdle	

Activity	Purpose	Curriculum links: *England* / Scotland

◎ Practise this move, taking turns to 'tip the wheelbarrow'.

1a, 1b, 2a, 2b, 2c, 8a, 8b
2a, 3a, 3b, 5a, 5b

Cool-down

◎ Children lie on their tummies, with their heads resting on their forearms. Then:

    slowly raise the right leg, hold and count to 5;

    slowly raise the left leg, hold and count to 5;

    gently push trunk up on extended arms, hold and count to 5;

    rest head on arms and count to 5.

Extension exercises stretch and relax muscles.

1a, 1b, 2a, 2b, 2c
1b, 2a

Recap   *3a, 3b, 3c, 4a, 4b*   1b, 2a, 3a, 6a

- Discuss why it might be important to try to balance on your hands. Refer to advanced gymnastic skills such as performing handstands or cartwheels, and jumping over vaults or horses.

- Also discuss the need to have strong shoulders – to write on the blackboard or whiteboard, to hold the ropes accurately when skipping, to place objects on top of cupboards or to construct a model.

- Can the children suggest how other animals move and what makes them different from each other?

- This lesson will be particularly tiring, owing to the effort in lifting the body's weight. Discuss effort and load.

Additional differentiation

- Encourage children who have restricted mobility to work from the floor, using a small range of movement in crawling. Adapt animals to accommodate ability – e.g. choose a hippopotamus with slow deliberate movements rather than bunny hops, and accept a commando crawl where a bunny hop is inappropriate.

- When attempting wheelbarrows, allow a child with limited upper-limb strength to shuffle on their lower arms and elbows with their upper legs supported, rather than extended arms with feet supported as in a traditional wheelbarrow position.

Objectives:

✻ to enhance awareness of deep pressure through the upper and lower limbs;

✻ to increase strength in upper and lower limbs;

✻ to maintain postural control against resistance.

Equipment:

✻ marking tape or chalk;

✻ sand bag (approx. 20–30cm) or other similar-sized soft bag filled with something heavy;

✻ flexible hoops (e.g. Polymat EverHoops) or skipping ropes.

Lesson summary

Warm-up: Wall press-ups	5 mins
Half press-ups	5 mins
Push o' war: upper limbs	5 mins
Single-handed push o' war	5 mins
Push o' war: lower limbs	5 mins
Dam busters	5–10 mins
Cool-down	5 mins
Recap	

Activity	Purpose	Curriculum links: *England / Scotland*
Warm-up: Wall press-ups ◎ Children stand approximately 1m from a wall. They place both palms on the wall at shoulder height, then bend their arms to lean forwards until their nose is touching the wall. They straighten their arms again to push away from the wall. ◎ Attempt 5–10 wall press-ups. ◎ This activity could also be called 'Rudolph' because if the child is able to get their nose to touch the wall several times, it may look pink – like Rudolph the Red-nosed Reindeer's!	Warming up the muscles surrounding the shoulder girdle	*1a, 1b, 2b, 2c, 8a* *1b, 2a*
Half press-ups ◎ Revisit the half press-ups from Lesson 29. ◎ Children attempt 5 press-ups.	Warming up the shoulder and hip muscles against gravity	*1a, 1b, 2b, 2c, 8a, 8b* *2a, 6a*
Push o' war: upper limbs ◎ Children get into pairs. They place their palms together, and try to push each other across the room. No jerky movements are allowed. ◎ The winner is the player who succeeds in pushing their opponent across the room. ◎ Have several rounds of this game.	Effort comes from the legs, but pressure is applied through the arms.	*1a, 1b, 2b, 2c, 8a* *2b, 3a, 5a, 6a*
Single-handed push o' war ◎ As above, but using the right hand only; the other arm is kept behind the back. ◎ Attempt 2–4 times.	Encourages effort through the lower limbs, while providing deep pressure through the upper limb which is also crossing the midline of the body	*1a, 1b, 2b, 2c, 8a* *2b, 3a, 5a, 6a*

Activity	Purpose	Curriculum links: *England* / Scotland

Push o' war: lower limbs

◎ In pairs again, children sit on the floor opposite each other with their legs straight and the soles of the feet touching. With their knees slightly bent and using the arms to push, they attempt to push each other across the room.

◎ Attempt 2–4 times.

Effort comes from the upper limbs but pressure is applied through the legs.

1a, 1b, 2b, 2c, 8a, 8b
2b, 3a, 5a, 6a

Dam busters

◎ Mark a starting line at one side of the room and a parallel finishing line approx. 10m away.

◎ Put the class into 6 teams of 4 or 5. Position half of each team behind the starting line and the remaining half behind the finishing line – ready for a team relay race.

◎ Place one sand bag (or other weighted bag) in front of the first player from each team.

Effort is coming from both lower limbs and extended arms.

Deep pressure is experienced through extended arms.

◎ Each team member must push the weighted bag from across to the line opposite, whereupon the next player pushes it back again. This continues until all team members have pushed the bag across.

◎ Players can crawl and push using both hands or alternate hands.

1a, 1b, 2b, 2c, 8a, 8b
3a, 3b, 5a

Cool-down

◎ Children get into pairs and sit on the floor opposite each other, as for Push o' war: lower limbs. Provide each pair with a flexible hoop (or skipping rope).

◎ Children hold onto the hoop and slowly lean back, stretching the hoop as far as possible (without lying on the floor). They hold this position for 10 seconds, then return to sitting position.

◎ Repeat 5 times.

◎ They attempt this same movement with their eyes closed.

◎ Control the pace of movement and length of hold.

Slow stretching action

1a, 1b, 2b, 2c, 8a, 8b
1b, 2a, 3a, 5a

Recap   *3a, 3b, 3c, 4a, 4b*   1b, 2a, 6a

- Discuss which part of the body was using the most energy in tasks such as Push o' war (hands or feet).

- Explain why it is important to apply pressure through the limbs. It provides our brain with a mental map of where our limbs are in relation to our body. Explain that this mental map helps us when we need to do something with our arms or legs without looking at them. Consider a few examples: combing our hair, cleansing after using the toilet, tying an apron, eating our tea while watching the TV, operating computer game controls while looking at the screen. Can the children think of others?

- Does anyone have difficulty doing things without looking?

Additional differentiation

- Be very careful during this session that movements are not jerky and that pressure is smooth and gradual.

- In Push o' war, children who have increased muscle tone should attempt to remain in a selected position rather than actively moving their partner with force, as this may increase spasticity.

Objectives:

✳ to develop strength in upper limbs;

✳ to stimulate deep muscle sensation to improve motor control;

✳ to enjoy simple team games incorporating pulling activities.

Equipment:

✳ old blankets, or sheets or towels;

✳ marking tape or chalk;

✳ flexible hoop (e.g. Polymat EverHoop) or large rubber quoit;

✳ CD player and music such as 'The locomotion' or a conga.

It is important that a polished floor is available for this session.

Lesson summary	
Warm-up: Human bop-it	5 mins
Tug o' war	5 mins
Blanket slide	5 mins
Blanket rollercoaster	5–10 mins
Human tug o' war	10 mins
Cool-down	5 mins
Recap	

Activity	**Purpose** **Curriculum links:** *England* / Scotland
Warm-up: Human bop-it ◎ Children imagine they are the game Bop-It (a hand-held electronic action game), which gives a command such as twist it, flick it, pull it – which you must act upon within a couple of seconds to win. Perform the following actions: 　Bop it – slap the floor. 　Twist it – twist at trunk (keep feet in one position). 　Pull it – hold hands together and pull outwards. 　Spin it – spin around. 　Flick it – kick legs sideways. ◎ Try to catch children out by increasing the speed of directions.	Warming up the muscles which will be used in pulling activities *1a, 1b, 2a, 2b, 2c, 8a, 8b* *1a, 2a, 2b, 3b*
Tug o' war ◎ Children get into pairs. They start in the middle of the room, holding each other's hands or wrists. Each child then tries to pull their partner gently across the room (without jerky movements). ◎ Change pairs. Pull each partner across the room 2–4 times.	Developing upper-limb strength against resistance Stimulating deep pressure receptors in upper- and lower-limb muscles *1a, 1b, 2a, 2b, 2c, 8a, 8b* *3a, 4b, 5a, 5b*
Blanket slide ◎ Put children into groups of 3. Give each group an old blanket (or towel or sheet). ◎ One child sits on the blanket while the other two slide them across the room. ◎ Children change places. Each child crosses the room on the blanket twice.	Enhancing muscle strength while stimulating muscle proprioceptors *1a, 1b, 2a, 2b, 2c, 8a, 8b* *2a, 3a, 4b, 5a, 5b*

Activity	Purpose	Curriculum links: *England* / Scotland
Blanket rollercoaster ◎ Encourage the children to think of different and unusual ways of moving their passenger across the room using the blanket – e.g. the passenger could lie on the blanket, the slide could zig-zag across the room, or they could alter the speed. ◎ Each child should cross the room on the blanket at least once. Share ideas with the rest of the class.	Encouraging creativity Inventing new ways of travelling, which also incorporates pulling a load	*1a, 1b, 2a, 2b, 2c, 8c, 8d* 4a, 4b, 5a, 5b
Human tug o' war ◎ Put the class into two teams. Make a central mark on the floor and two smaller marks approximately 1m from the centre. ◎ Each team makes a human rope by holding onto the waist of the child in front. The two teams face each other end-on and the children at the front of each rope hold onto opposite sides of a flexible hoop (or large rubber quoit). ◎ On the word 'Go', each team tries to pull the other rope over to their side of the marker. ◎ Repeat 2 or 3 times with different teams, e.g. boys versus girls.	Group cooperation Group resistance	*1a, 1b, 2a, 2b, 2c, 8a, 8b* 3a, 5a
Cool-down ◎ Children sit on the floor in the same teams as Human tug o' war, but seated between each other's legs, in a line. ◎ Cool down by singing a couple of raps or songs such as 'The locomotion', which involves rocking forwards and back, and side to side, in synchrony.	Calming activity which requires rocking motion, side to side and front to back	*1a, 1b, 2a, 2b, 2c, 8a, 8b, 8c* 1b, 2a, 5a

Recap   *3a, 3b, 3c, 4a, 4b*   1b, 2a, 6a

- Compare this lesson's activities, which involved pulling, with the previous lesson's, which required pushing. Which were easier, and why? (Pushing is usually easier as you have the force of your body weight to help with the effort.)

- How did being pulled on the blanket feel? How might the movement change if the floor surface differed?

Additional differentiation

- During Blanket slide and Blanket rollercoaster, either place a child with restricted mobility on the blanket, or attach the corner of the blanket to the wheelchair to assist with the 'pull' action.

- Nominate the child with restricted mobility as judge in Human tug o' war; the movements incorporated into this activity may become jerky and cause imbalance.

Area: *Gymnastic activities*

Objectives:

✱ to enhance body awareness by stimulating touch receptors;

✱ to improve motor coordination by increasing the awareness of limb position;

✱ to increase observation skills in order to refine motor control.

Equipment:

✱ prepared list of spatial concepts;

✱ CD player and music.

Lesson summary

Warm-up: Musical concepts	5 mins
Rub-a-dub-dub	5 mins
Copy-cats	10 mins
Mirror moves	5 mins
Body shapes	5 mins
Letter shapes	10 mins
Cool-down	5 mins
Recap	

Activity	Purpose — Curriculum links: *England* / Scotland
Warm-up: Musical concepts ◎ Have ready a list of words and phrases related to spatial concepts, some of which mean the same thing, e.g. beneath and under. Include concepts such as left, right, behind, in front, adjacent, beneath, under, inside, outside, on top, over, next to, near. ◎ Children get into pairs. ◎ Play some music and encourage the children to move around according to the rhythm. When the music stops, call out a concept such as 'beside', at which children must place themselves in a suitable position – in this instance, next to their partner. ◎ Explain any terms which are unfamiliar to children.	Providing an opportunity to assess children's understanding of basic spatial concepts including laterality *1a, 1b, 2a, 2b, 2c* 1a, 2a, 2b, 3a, 3b, 5a
Rub-a-dub-dub ◎ Children stimulate their limbs by rubbing different parts of the body, starting gently but increasing vigour. Massage parts in the following order: face, neck, arms, chest, tummy, arms, hands, thighs and lower legs. ◎ Finally, stamp the feet.	Stimulating the body's touch receptors and proprioceptors (these are receptors located in the joints and muscles which provide an accurate picture of where the limbs are in relation to the body) *1a* 1a, 1b, 2a
Copy-cats ◎ Children get into pairs. Encourage the children to mirror each other's movements, taking it in turns to take the lead. Include both arm and leg movements – e.g. the leader might balance on their right leg and count to 3, then twirl around before jumping on the spot twice. ◎ Each child takes their turn to lead – approx. 3 minutes each.	The stimulation caused by increasing deep sensation should enhance the child's observation skills and awareness of limb position. *1a, 1b, 2a, 2b, 2c, 8c* 2a, 3a, 3b, 4b, 5a, 5b

Activity	Purpose	Curriculum links: *England /* Scotland
Mirror moves ◎ Children change partners and again mirror each other's movements, this time incorporating movement around the room. Pairs should keep very close to each other. ◎ Each child takes a turn to lead – approx. 3 minutes each.	Encouraging observation while moving	*1a, 1b, 2a, 2b, 2c, 8c* 2a, 2b, 3a, 3b, 4b, 5a, 5b
Body shapes ◎ Children change partners again. Together, using their whole bodies, they create the shapes you call out. Ask for circles, squares, rectangles, triangles, diamonds and stars. ◎ Ask each pair to select a shape of their choice and demonstrate it to the rest of the class. Can the class guess what the shape is?	Enhancing body awareness	*1a, 1b, 2a, 2b, 2c, 8b, 8c* 2a, 3a, 4a, 4b, 5b
Letter shapes ◎ Change partners again, and this time children choose a letter and together make the shape with their bodies. ◎ Pairs display their shapes to the rest of the class, who try to guess the letter. ◎ Initially you may need to direct children to produce specific letters that encourage collaboration: w, m, h are good for this.	Developing accurate body awareness Encouraging cooperative learning *1a, 1b, 2a, 2b, 2c, 8b, 8c* 4b, 4c, 5a, 5b	
Cool-down ◎ Children find a space on the floor and lie down. Slowly, they spell out their name using their body. ◎ Ask selected children to demonstrate, if appropriate.	Developing careful body control *1a, 1b, 2a, 2b, 2c* 3a, 5b	

Recap   *3a, 3b, 3c, 4a, 4b*   1b, 6a

- Ask children why they started the session by rubbing all over their bodies. Explain that this is to wake up their muscles and stimulate the little triggers which lie under their skin and help them to know where their arms and legs are without needing to look at them.
- Discuss how they used their bodies to copy their partners, and which movements were hard and which easy.
- Discuss their choices of shape and letter. Why did they choose the letters they selected? Is it harder to make your body into a round or straight shape?

Area: *Gymnastic activities*

Objectives:
✳ to develop an awareness of how the body moves;

✳ to develop motor control and balance;

✳ to develop an accurate body image.

Equipment:
✳ a series of 3- or 4-lettered words written on cards
   (if working with very young children).

Lesson summary
Warm-up: Pass the …	5 mins
Who started it?	5–10 mins
People to people	10 mins
More letter shapes	5 mins
Body words	10 mins
Cool-down	5 mins
Recap	

Activity	Purpose	Curriculum links: *England* / Scotland
Warm-up: Pass the … ◎ Children stand in a circle, or several smaller circles (6–8 children), depending on the class size. ◎ Ask a child to start by squeezing the hand of the person next to them briefly. That child in turn passes the squeeze to the next person, and so on until the squeeze has gone full circle. ◎ Do the same with other actions, e.g. hugs, high 5s, rubs and pats. Encourage the children to think of an action to pass on. ◎ Do approx. 5 circuits, depending on group size. Increase the number of circuits if groups are small.	Developing observation skills and anticipation Stimulating tactile sensation	*1a, 1b, 2a, 2b, 2c* 2a, 3b, 5a, 5b
Who started it? ◎ Children remain in the circle or circles. Choose a child to withdraw for a moment. Then choose one of the remaining circle members to lead, by starting a rhythm or an action – e.g. using a click, clap, slap, stamp or kick. ◎ The withdrawn child is brought back and stands in the middle of the circle as an observer. The circle leader begins with an action which everyone else in the circle must copy and keep going. After a few seconds, when the action has become established, the leader changes the action. ◎ The observer must try to guess who is leading the action. Only 3 guesses are allowed. ◎ Change observers and circle leaders, and repeat several times.	This activity encourages detailed observation while simultaneously developing limb awareness through motion and tactile stimuli.	*1a, 1b, 2a, 2b, 2c* 3a, 4a, 5a, 5b

Activity	Purpose	Curriculum links: England / Scotland
People to people ◎ Put the children into pairs. Call out an action which requires them to negotiate a position requiring movement and balance; e.g. 2 hands and 2 feet on the floor; elbow to ear; knee to chin. ◎ Children must quickly get into these positions and retain them until the teacher has observed their accuracy. ◎ After 5 instructions, call 'People to people', at which everyone must find a new partner. ◎ If appropriate, this may be made into a competition by removing the last pair to position themselves in each round.	Developing negotiation skills This activity can test a child's coordination and balance while improving body awareness.	*1a, 1b, 2a, 2b, 2c, 8b* *3a, 4b, 5a*
More letter shapes ◎ As preparation for the next activity, briefly revisit Letter shapes from lesson 33: children choose a letter and together make the shape with their bodies. Pairs display their letters to the rest of the class to guess.	This activity serves to remind the children of the activity which was introduced during the preceding lesson, and to help them use their whole body to express shape and form.	*1a, 1b, 2a, 2b, 2c, 8b* *4b, 4c, 5a, 5b*
Body words ◎ Join pairs together to make groups of 4. Ask children to think of a 3- or 4-letter word and to spell this out using their bodies. Each group may do up to 3 words. ◎ Each group presents their word to the rest of the class to guess. ◎ If working with very young children, have a few word cards (e.g. top, car, curl). 	Developing negotiation skills and enhancing body awareness	*1a, 1b, 2a, 2b, 2c, 8b* *3a, 4a, 4b, 5a, 5b*
Cool-down ◎ The children lie down in a space. You call out a selection of letters which they must try to position themselves into. Emphasise that control rather than speed is important.	Controlled concluding activity	*1a, 1b, 2a, 2b, 2c* *2a, 4a*

Recap   *3a, 3b, 3c, 4a, 4b*   *6a*

- Discuss the importance of observation skills in helping to improve motor control and balance.

- Refer to the importance of observation in appreciating how others are feeling.

- Emphasise that relationships are dependent on empathy and negotiation.

- Discuss the term 'negotiation' in relation to the last exercise, which involved organisation and collaboration.

Lesson 35

Action sequences 1

Area: *Gymnastic activities*

Objectives:

✳ to develop acute observation skills;

✳ to memorise sequences of movements;

✳ to make timely movements.

Equipment:

✳ CD player and rock and roll music.

Lesson summary

Warm-up: Body jive	5 mins
Mexican wave	5 mins
Chinese knots	5–10 mins
Sequential memory	5–10 mins
I like to …	5–10 mins
Cool-down	5 mins
Recap	

Activity	Purpose	Curriculum links: *England* / Scotland
Warm-up: Body jive ◎ Play some lively pop music and lead the class in a warm-up which incorporates a hand jive, shoulder shimmies and high kicks. ◎ Suggested music: 'You ain't nothing but a hound dog', 'The hippy, hippy shake'.	Warming up all the muscles while developing rhythm and observation skills	*1a, 1b, 2a, 2b, 2c* 1a, 1b, 3a, 3b
Mexican wave ◎ Children form either one large circle or several smaller circles. ◎ Select a child to start a Mexican wave, in which each child stretches down to the toes and up in the air in sequence.	Developing observation skills, timing, and stretching ability	*1a, 1b, 2a, 2b, 2c, 8b* 3a, 5a
Chinese knots ◎ Children form circles of approx. 8–10. Ask one child to step out of the circle to be the puzzle-solver. (Select a child who will be able to give good verbal instructions to the others.) ◎ All remaining children in the circle hold hands and create a group knot. They do this by actions such as stepping over arms, crouching under a pair of legs, and threading legs over a pair's arms. It is vital, however, that the hands remain held. ◎ The puzzle-solver must try to disentangle the knot by separating hands at one point only, then giving directions to straighten out the group. ◎ Do 3 knots. 	Enhancing body awareness while promoting muscle resistance and stamina	*1a, 1b, 2a, 2b, 2c, 8b* 3a, 4b, 5a, 5b

Activity	Purpose	Curriculum links: *England* / Scotland
Sequential memory	Developing observation, memory and movement	
◉ Put children into groups of 6–8. Groups sit in circles. Ask one child in the group to think of and then perform a sequence of movements.		
◉ The second person in the group must then remember and repeat these to the third child, and so on until all members have repeated the movement sequence.		
◉ At the end, ask the first child whether the original sequence has changed in any way.		*1a, 1b, 2a, 2b, 2c, 8c, 8d* 3b, 4a, 5a, 5b
I like to …	Developing memory of a sequence of movements	
This is a movement variation on the traditional game, I went to market.		
◉ Children remain in groups of 6–8 and stand in a circle.		
◉ Each group starts to clap in rhythm. The first child says, 'My name is … and I like to …', and does a move to complete the sentence; e.g. 3 claps, 2 clicks, a stamp, a spin, a hop, a roll.		
◉ The next child must recall the sentence, remember the original action and add another. The game continues in the same way. Each action or movement must be different. Each child tries to recall as many actions in the correct order as possible.		
◉ Play once round the group.		*1a, 1b, 2a, 2b, 2c, 8b, 8c* 3b, 4a, 4b, 5a, 5b
Cool-down	Calming final activity	
◉ Ask all children to remember as many actions as possible from the previous game, and perform these individually – slowly, and with control.		*1a, 1b, 2a, 2b, 2c, 8c, 8d* 2a, 3b, 6a

Recap   *3a, 3b, 3c, 4a, 4b*   3b, 4a, 6a

- Discuss the importance of observation and memory when learning a sequence of movements. Ask the children to say what strategies they used to help them remember the sequences.

- What other sequences do the children have to remember? Refer to spelling, putting on their clothes in the right order, numbers in maths, etc.

Action sequences 2

Area: *Gymnastic activities*

Objectives:

✴ to develop sequential memory;

✴ to provide cues to help aid recall;

✴ to develop spatial planning and organisation.

Equipment:

✴ marking tape or chalk;

✴ 4 gym benches.

Lesson summary

Warm-up: Sequence rap	5 mins
Sequence race	10 mins
Up and down sequences	10 mins
Bench organisation game	10 mins
Cool-down	5–10 mins

Activity	Purpose	Curriculum links: *England* / Scotland
Warm-up: Sequence rap ◉ Start a sequence of claps for all the children to copy. Then incorporate stamping and jumping. ◉ Gradually extend the length of sequence for the children to recall.	Introducing the concept of recalling simple sequences	*1a, 1b, 2a, 2b, 2c, 8d* 1a, 3b
Sequence race ◉ Put the class into 4–6 teams. Create starting and finishing lines. ◉ Demonstrate a simple sequence which the children must use to cross the room to the finishing line. Start with a very simple one, e.g. 4 strides, 4 hops. ◉ Team members take turns to race across the room following the sequence. On reaching the finishing line, they run back to the team, and the next team member sets off, following the sequence. ◉ Have 2–6 races, increasing the complexity of sequences according to the ability of class members – e.g. you might end up with 4 hops, 4 jumps, 4 turns and 4 skips. You could vary the number of the moves for a more complex sequence – e.g. 4 jumps, 2 skips and 1 turn.	Developing sequential organisation Providing opportunity for observation of children's sequential memory skills	*1a, 1b, 2a, 2b, 2c, 8d* 3b, 5a
Up and down sequences ◉ Set up as for the previous race, but place 2–4 gym benches across the room as obstacles. ◉ Ask the children to follow a sequence of movement which includes up and down movements, e.g. 4 steps on toes, 4 moves on knees. ◉ Children then have to cross the room using the sequence, negotiating the obstacles (gym benches) in the way. ◉ Do 4 races.	Providing opportunity for observation of ability to adhere to sequential memory when distractions are present	*1a, 1b, 2a, 2b, 2c, 8d* 3a, 3b, 5a

Activity	Purpose	Curriculum links: *England* / Scotland

Bench organisation game

◎ Create teams of 4. Stand the first team on a low bench and ask them to arrange themselves in order according to age, without falling off the bench.

◎ Let the other 3 teams take their turn on the bench.

◎ The winners are the team who succeed in rearranging their order accurately without falling off the bench.

◎ Teams could be asked to order themselves according to:

hair colour – from darkest to lightest;

house number;

number of siblings;

favourite number;

height.

◎ If two children have the same feature, they simply stand next to each other.

Developing group co-operation, teamwork and trust

Encouraging accurate spatial planning, organisation and action

1a, 1b, 2a, 2b, 2c, 8a, 8b
3a, 5a

Cool-down

◎ Children remain in groups of 4. You give a series of actions relating to what is touching the floor, e.g.:

4 feet on the floor plus 2 hands;

3 feet and 4 hands;

4 bottoms and 4 feet;

6 knees and 6 hands.

◎ The group must discuss and plan how they are going to achieve each position before getting themselves into it.

Group co-operation and balance

1a, 1b, 2a, 2b, 2c, 8a
2a, 5a, 5b, 6a

Recap   *3a, 3b, 3c, 4a, 4b*   *3b, 6a*

- Discuss sequential memory. How many children think they are good at remembering things? Can anyone remember their telephone number? How did they learn this?

- Discuss the fact that sometimes having a physical prompt can help you to remember things more easily.

- Can children think of other activities or lessons where they have to remember a series of things, e.g. spellings, maths rules (times tables)? Explain that today's lesson helps with this.

Additional differentiation

- Children with restricted mobility should initially stay in their wheelchairs. The Sequence race can be adapted by the creation of an individual sequence, e.g. propel forward for a count of 4, rotate chair, propel forward for a count of 4, rotate chair.

- They can manoeuvre around obstacles in the Up and down sequences.

- They could transfer out of the wheelchair for the Bench organisation game and have support at the hips to sit on the bench. The child must then shuffle to the left or right (as appropriate), and the rest of the team will step over the child without toppling. A supportive peer will be essential to help with this. Ensure that only one move is necessary for the child, rather than having to pass by 3 others.

Assessment of space 1

Area: *Gymnastic activities*

Objectives:

✳ to develop spatial planning and organisation;

✳ to develop coordinated movements;

✳ to develop assessment and approximation.

Equipment:

✳ up to 20 adult-sized shoe boxes;

✳ stopwatch;

✳ 2 or 3 full-length ladders (or marking tape or chalk);

✳ recording sheets for estimation game which incorporate 2 columns, one for estimation and another for actual amount (use these for discussion later);

✳ pencils.

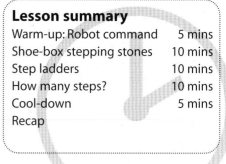

Lesson summary

Warm-up: Robot command	5 mins
Shoe-box stepping stones	10 mins
Step ladders	10 mins
How many steps?	10 mins
Cool-down	5 mins
Recap	

Activity	Purpose	Curriculum links: *England* / Scotland
Warm-up: Robot command ◉ Children imagine they are robots which you operate by remote control. You can give the commands: forwards, backwards, sideways, turn around, slow, fast. Children must obey the commands, keeping their arms and legs straight.	Moving with varying speeds Coordinate movements within a restricted space without collision	*1a, 1b, 2a, 2b, 2c, 8a* 1a, 2a, 2b
Shoe-box stepping stones ◉ Place a series of adult-sized shoe boxes across the room, end to end, approx. 5cm apart. ◉ Children must carefully cross the room by placing their feet inside each box, imagining each as a stepping stone. If the floor is touched, the child has fallen into the river and must return to the start. ◉ After each child has crossed, form teams and time the teams crossing the room using the stepping stones.	Foot placement and spatial planning Balance and coordination	*1a, 1b, 2a, 2b, 2c, 8a, 8b* 2a, 2b, 3a, 3b
Step ladders ◉ Place 2 or 3 full-length ladders on the floor. (If these are not available, use marking tape to create 4m ladders or use chalk to create them in the playground.) ◉ Children must cross the room by carefully placing their feet between the rungs of the ladder and crossing over from one ladder to the next to reach the opposite side.	Developing controlled motor and spatial planning	

Activity	Purpose	Curriculum links: *England* / Scotland
◎ Once this has been performed individually, create small groups of 4 or 5 children who must cross the room on the ladders, holding hands throughout. ◎ The goal is not speed but teamwork. If this activity is done at speed, errors will occur and the children will probably overbalance.		*1a, 1b, 2a, 2b, 2c, 8a, 8b* 2a, 2b, 3a, 3b, 5a

How many steps?
 	
◎ Children get into pairs. One of each pair names an object in the room and says, 'How many steps will it take you to reach the [name of the object]?' Their partner must estimate the number of steps, and then walk to the object.
 	
◎ Pairs may record their estimations and results, to assess the accuracy of their estimation.
 	
◎ As alternatives, try:
    How many hands?
    How many forearms (elbow to tip of middle finger)?
    How many footprints (heel to toe measurement)?
    How many hops?
	Accurate assessment of space
	Accurate assessment of body schema
	Visual figure–ground discrimination
		1a, 1b, 2a, 2b, 2c, 8a
		4a, 5a, 5b

Cool-down: What's the time, Mr Wolf? ◎ Choose a child to play the wolf. They stand almost at the end of one side of the room with their back to the rest of the class. ◎ The rest of the class must try to cross to the opposite side of the room, creeping carefully past the wolf. As they do this, they call, 'What's the time, Mr Wolf?' The wolf responds with a time, e.g. 'One o'clock.' Children creep forward according to the number called – in this instance, 1 step forward. ◎ At any time the wolf can respond to the question by shouting 'Dinner time!', at which everyone must run to avoid being captured. All those captured by the wolf must either join the wolf family, or sit out. ◎ Use different ways of moving across the room, e.g. hopping, skipping, slithering, jumping and side-stepping.	Auditory discrimination Approximation of distance Controlled movements	*1a, 1b, 2a, 2b, 2c, 8a, 8b* 2a, 2b, 3a, 5b

Recap   *3a, 3b, 3c, 4a, 4b*   4b, 6a

- Discuss how today's activities required children to guess or estimate distances, emphasising the importance of this in everyday movement. Use examples such as crossing the road, avoiding obstacles on pavements, manoeuvring around tight corners or around cluttered classrooms.

- Ask the children if anyone has ever had an accident because they didn't accurately judge the space around them. Did they knock something over, or trip up or hurt someone else?

- Discuss how estimation is important for guessing distances, numbers, amounts, weights, and working out how many words to write on a line or whether there is enough space to write a word. Refer to mathematics, science and literacy.

- Spend some time looking at the record sheets from How many steps?, considering how close children's estimations were to the actual distances.

Assessment of space 2

Area: *Gymnastic activities*

Objectives:

✱ to develop spatial planning;

✱ to observe individual ability to judge distances at speed;

✱ to increase motor-response time.

Equipment:

✱ 1 or 2 handkerchiefs;

✱ marking tape or chalk;

✱ sheets of A4 paper – enough for 2 sheets for each child;

✱ 12 coloured hula hoops and hoop stands (or, e.g., Polymat EverHoops, which have stands);

✱ 12 tall cones.

Lesson summary

Warm-up: All change	5 mins
Hanky tag	5 mins
Stepping stones relay	5–10 mins
Hills and holes	10 mins
Human obstacle course	5–10 mins
Cool-down	5 mins
Recap	

Activity	Purpose	Curriculum links: *England / Scotland*
Warm-up: All change ◎ Children run round the room as you command. Incorporate changes in direction, speed, plane and action (e.g. hopping, 2-feet jumping, skipping).	Gradually warming up muscles ready for active games	1a, 1b, 2a, 2b, 2c 1a, 1b, 2a, 2b
Hanky tag ◎ Children sit on the floor in a large circle. One child walks around the circle carrying a handkerchief. When the hanky is dropped next to a child, that child must jump up, grab the hanky and try to catch the person who dropped it. ◎ If they catch them, they can return to their own seat; if they don't, they become the hanky dropper. ◎ If the group is large, have two hanky droppers in action.	Anticipating and achieving a rapid response	1a, 1b, 2a, 2b, 8a 3a, 3b, 5a
Stepping stones relay ◎ Create a starting line and a finishing line (the distance depends on the ability of the children). ◎ Put the class into 4–6 teams. Give each child two sheets of A4 paper (this can be rough or used paper). ◎ The first team member has to cross from the start to the finishing line, using the two pieces of paper as stepping stones. This involves placing a sheet of paper on the floor, stepping on it, placing another sheet ahead of the first, stepping onto that piece, retrieving the first sheet and so on. Continue to the finishing line. ◎ Once across, the child runs back to their team and the next child sets off, with their own stepping stones. ◎ If a child falls off a stone, they must return to the beginning. ◎ Do a practice run before introducing a competitive element or participation at speed.	Coordinated movements Accurate spatial planning and execution	1a, 1b, 2a, 2b, 8a, 8b 3a, 3b, 5a

Activity	Purpose	Curriculum links:
		England / Scotland

Hills and holes

◎ Put the class into teams of approx. 8. Put a row of alternating hula hoops and tall cones across the room.

◎ On the word 'Go', the first child in each team must crawl through each hoop, then step over each cone, as quickly as possible. When they reach the finishing line, they run back and tag the next person on their team to indicate their turn.

Imaginatively organising the environment to incorporate variations in planes of movement and space

1a, 1b, 2a, 2b, 8a, 8b
3a, 3b, 4b, 5a

Human obstacle course

◎ Children stay in teams. Designate a team director for each team.

◎ Each team has to create an obstacle course out of team members, who shape their bodies into bridges to travel under, boulders to step over, arches to go through, and so on.

◎ Teams take turns to try to complete each other's courses, under the direction of the team director. Penalties are given for any collisions.

Moulding the body into a series of shapes

This task requires children to develop controlled balance and spatial organisation.

1a, 1b, 2a, 2b, 8a, 8b, 8c
3a, 3b, 4b, 5a

Cool-down

◎ Individually, children devise a sequence of movements which incorporates stretches, balances on one leg, rolls, turns and twists.

◎ They run through their sequence at slow speed.

Concluding activity to draw the group together at the end of the session

1a, 1b, 2a, 2b
2a, 4a

Recap   *3a, 3b, 3c, 4a, 4b   5a, 6a*

- Was it difficult to perform today's activities without bumping into each other? Why? What precautions did you have to use to prevent collisions?

- What was the hardest thing about the Stepping stones game? Could you balance and simultaneously move the stones?

- How did you decide on the format for Human obstacle course? Could you practise these activities outside school?

Additional differentiation

- Allow children with restricted mobility to play Hanky tag from their wheelchair, with all class members sitting on chairs in a circle, rather than on the floor.
- Modify the Stepping stones activity so that, rather than stepping on the stones, the child must carefully weave in and out of these. If anyone complains that this is easy, ask them to have a go!

Lesson 39

Assessment of space 3

Area: *Gymnastic activities*

Objectives:

✷ to develop spatial organisation;

✷ to increase tactile sensation which enhances body image;

✷ to develop group cooperation and teamwork.

Equipment:

✷ gym mats;

✷ hula hoops – 1 for each child;

✷ hoop stands (or use Polymat EverHoops, which have stands);

✷ 2 or 3 gym benches;

✷ short cones;

✷ tall cones;

✷ rubber arrows (e.g. Directional Arrows™) or marking tape;

✷ a few beanbags.

Lesson summary

Warm-up: Movement circus	5–10 mins
Sharks	10 mins
Thread the buckle	5 mins
Bear hunt	5 mins
Excuse me	10 mins
Cool-down	5 mins
Recap	

Activity	Purpose	Curriculum links: *England / Scotland*
Warm-up: Movement circus ◎ Children carry out each of the following activities on matting once or twice: bottom walking (sit on the floor with legs straight and arms folded, and retaining folded arms bottom shuffle across room) – a race may be incorporated; rolling (sideways, with the body straight); rolling (forwards; children should be encouraged to perform forward rolls on the gym mats if possible); back-to-back standing (pairs of children stand back-to-back, with elbows interlocked; they attempt to sit down and stand up together); back swings (in the same position as above, children gently bend forward so their partners are stretched and balanced on their back, with the tips of their toes remaining on the floor; the movement is reciprocated – children should be discouraged from lifting their partner's feet from the floor).	Developing deep sensory pressure in order to enhance the child's body awareness	*1a, 1b, 2a, 2b, 2c, 8a, 8b* *1a, 2a, 2b, 3a, 5a*

Activity	Purpose	Curriculum links: England / Scotland

Sharks

◎ Lay a series of hoops (the same number as there are children) on the floor – these are islands.

◎ Children swim around the islands, using their arms to depict breast-stroke, front crawl, butterfly or backstroke.

◎ When you shout 'Shark!', everyone must get onto an island. A hoop is then removed, and the game proceeds. The aim is not for anyone to be out, but for children to rescue their friends by sharing hoops.

◎ As hoops are removed, one at a time, several children will be squeezed into each circle. If children fall out of the island they are out.

◎ Children who are able to escape to the last island are the winners.

◎ Play 1 or 2 games.

Purpose: Developing assessment of space and team cooperation

1a, 1b, 2a, 2b, 2c, 8a, 8b
1a, 3a, 4b, 5a

Thread the buckle

◎ Create 3 or 4 groups of approx. 7 children. Ask each group to hold hands in a line. The first child in the group holds a hula hoop on their arm and must pass it over their body to the next person, without breaking the connection.

◎ After a practice run, this activity can be undertaken as a race.

Purpose: Developing balance and coordination, and teamwork

1a, 1b, 2a, 2b, 2c, 8a, 8b
3a, 4b, 5a

Bear hunt

◎ Create an obstacle course using gym benches with low cones placed on top, tall cones and hoops. Rubber arrows (or marking tape) can also be used to show direction.

◎ Children follow the trail individually, stepping over, on or through obstacles – as in the traditional story, 'We're going on a bear hunt'.

Purpose: Providing opportunity for observation of spatial organisation

◎ Create groups of 4–6 children to follow the trail for a second time, this time holding hands.

You could read the book *We're Going on a Bear Hunt*, by Michael Rosen, before this activity – and have paw prints rather than arrows to direct the group around the obstacle course.

1a, 1b, 2a, 2b, 2c, 8a, 8b
3a, 3b, 4c, 5a

Activity	Purpose	Curriculum links: _England_ / Scotland
Excuse me ◉ Place 2 or 3 gym benches centrally in the room, and position a team of 5–8 children at each end of each bench. On the bench, place a series of beanbags and low cones to act as obstacles. ◉ The first members of the teams at each end of the bench must simultaneously climb onto the bench (at opposite ends) and attempt to step over each obstacle on the bench. They will inevitably meet in the centre, and must carefully negotiate a way past each other to get to the end. ◉ As they step off the bench at the end, the next player can start. In this way the teams should completely swap places. ◉ Run through the activity twice. The complexity of the obstacles can be increased or decreased according to the children's ages and abilities.	Developing spatial awareness while encouraging negotiation skills Extending balance skills	_8a, 8b, 8c_ 3b, 4b, 5a
Cool-down ◉ Bring the whole class together. Ask the children to organise themselves in a row according to their birthdays: January at one end of the room, December at the other. Try other arrangements, e.g. according to hair colour (darkest to lightest) or house number.	Assessing sequential organisation skills	_2c_ 4b, 5a

Recap   _3a, 3b, 3c, 4a, 4b_   6a

- Discuss how today's activities required considerable balance skills, strength and coordination, but above all an ability to work together.

- Which activities did the children find the hardest and why?

Additional differentiation

- Children who are wheelchair dependent can come out of their chair for warm-up activities. Modify the back-to-back standing and back swings by getting the children to sit on the floor, back to back, with arms interlocked, then to slide their partner by pushing with the feet.

- An alternative obstacle course can be provided for the child who is unable to move along the gym bench. A course which requires the skilful manoeuvring of a wheelchair may incorporate human obstacles. If time allows, others in the class can try this to demonstrate how difficult it can be to manoeuvre a wheelchair around obstacles.

Objectives:

❋ to apply deep pressure to stimulate kinaesthetic sense and heighten body schema;

❋ to apply effort through the hips and trunk in order to promote movement;

❋ to develop controlled rolling in a variety of directions and planes.

Equipment:

❋ marking tape or chalk;

❋ gym mats (or blankets).

Lesson summary

Warm-up: Animal antics	5 mins
Sausage-roll race	5 mins
Rafts ahoy!	5 mins
Ali Baba's escape	10 mins
Roly-poly overs	5–10 mins
Cool-down	5 mins
Recap	

Activity	Purpose	Curriculum links: *England* / Scotland
Warm-up: Animal antics ◉ Children try each of the following actions: sleeping hamsters – curl up into a tiny ball; caterpillars – stretch out on tummy, draw up knees and arms, and stretch down again; wiggly worms – roll sideways on the floor; stretching cats – curl up to one side, stretch, curl up again, and then stretch again on the opposite side.	Curling, rolling and twisting motion	*1a, 1b, 2a, 2b, 2c, 8b* 1a, 2b, 3a, 3b, 4a
Sausage-roll race ◉ Create a start and finishing line. Put the class into 4 teams. ◉ In turn each team member must roll across the room to the finishing line. Once the finishing line has been reached, the child runs back and tags the next player in their team to indicate their turn to start. ◉ Do a practice run and one race.	Developing ability to roll, which increases total body awareness through the stimulation of kinaesthetic and tactile receptors	*1a, 1b, 2a, 2b, 2c, 8b* 2a, 2b, 5a
Rafts ahoy! ◉ Children stay in 4 teams. This time all the team must roll across the room together, staying as close to each other as possible to give the appearance of a raft. ◉ The winning team are those who cross the sea, and manage to stay closest to each other. In this way, teamwork rather than speed is emphasised. ◉ Do a practice run and one race. 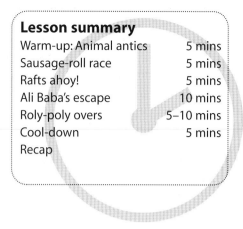	Increasing kinaesthetic and tactile sense while cooperating with team	*1a, 1b, 2a, 2b, 2c, 8b* 2a, 3a, 5a

Activity	Purpose	Curriculum links: *England* / Scotland

Ali Baba's escape

- Put the class into groups of 4. Provide each group with a soft gym mat (or blanket; soft gym mats provide more appropriate pressure and feedback than blankets).

- Select a child in each group to lie across the mat. The rest of the group gently roll them inside, leaving the head sticking out.

- The group then call out 'Ali Baba's escaped!' and the child unrolls from the mat, as fast as possible. Continue until each group member has had a turn at being Ali Baba.

This is an excellent activity for providing deep pressure to stimulate proprioception and tactile receptors.

1a, 1b, 2a, 2b, 2c, 8a, 8b
3a, 3b, 4a, 5a, 5b

Roly-poly overs

- Put the class into groups of 4 or 5.

- Each group has to find a way of crossing the room which incorporates twists, turns and forward, backward or sideways rolls. The most innovative team demonstrate, as an example.

- Mats can be used, if required for the group's routine.

Developing range of skills and actions

Enhancing kinaesthetic awareness

1a, 1b, 2a, 2b, 2c, 8a, 8b, 8d
4a, 4b, 5a, 5b

Cool-down

Play a game of Simon says, including forward rolls, backward rolls, twists, turns, side rolls and curls.

Concluding game which incorporates all movements made during today's lesson

1a, 1b, 2a, 2b, 2c
2a, 2b, 3a, 3b

Recap   *3a, 3b, 3c, 4a, 4b*   6a

- Was it difficult to keep the momentum up to roll across a distance? How many class members can perform a forward roll? What do you need to do to achieve this?

Equipment list

Item	In lesson	Low-cost alternative	Commercial product
arrows, rubber	39	marking tape	Directional Arrows™
ball	20		
balloons	10		
balls, soft, or shuttlecocks	11		
baseball bat, soft	11		
beach balls	8, 9	large round balloons	Spordas Super Duty Beach Balls™
beanbags	3, 5, 13, 14, 15, 18, 19, 23, 39		
blankets, sheets or towels, old	32		
buckets, large	14	storage containers	
cardboard fish	13		
cards, coloured	23		
carpet squares	25		
CD player	8, 23, 32, 33, 35		
chairs	3		
chalk	28		
clothes pegs, multi-coloured	20		
cones	2, 12, 16		
cones, short	17, 19, 29, 39		Super Safe Flexi Cones
cones, tall	38, 39		
crepe bandages or scarves	16		
cricket bat	4		
cricket stumps	11		
drum or tambourine	25, 27		
drum or tambourine or maracas	26		
foam balls, large	2, 4, 12, 15, 16, 17		

Item	In lesson	Low-cost alternative	Commercial product
foam balls, small	4, 5, 6		
foot shapes, plastic	24, 26	card foot shapes	Throw Down Hands and Feet
footballs	4, 15, 18		
footballs, Brazilian	18		
footballs, light	6		
frisbees, soft	7		Foam Flyers
goal	8	hula hoops or storage containers	Giant Go 4 Goal™
gym benches	36, 39		
gym mats	15, 19, 39, 40		
hand shapes, plastic	24	card hand shapes	Throw Down Hands and Feet
handkerchiefs	38		
hockey sticks, plastic indoor	16	narrow plastic pipe	Hok-E-Stik set™
hoops, flexible	32	rubber quoits	Polymat EverHoops
hoops, flexible	28, 31	skipping ropes	Polymat EverHoops
hoops, hula	7, 19, 20, 22, 26, 27, 38, 39		
hoops, hula	3	coloured mats	Spordas Space Stations™
hoop stands	38, 39		Spordas Expand-a-Hoop™ stand Polymat EverHoops (come with stands)
ladders	37	chalk- or tape-marked ladders	
marking tape or chalk	2, 3, 4, 5, 7, 8, 9, 10, 11, 12, 13, 14, 15, 16, 17, 18, 20, 24, 27, 31, 32, 36, 38, 40		
mats or carpet squares, coloured	23	card	Spordas Space Stations™
mini-beasts, plastic	24		
net, volleyball	9		Qwik Net™
nets, adjustable target	5	large buckets	Tippin Targets™
nets, low	10, 11		Qwik Net™

Item	In lesson	Low-cost alternative	Commercial product
nets, throw-and-catch	8	large towels	Spordas Fling-It™
newspapers, old	12, 13, 27		
paddle bats, small, or short-handled rackets	10, 11		
paper	37, 38		
pencils	37		
penny whistle, recorder or other wind instrument	1		
plates, paper or plastic	27		
Reflex soccer balls	18	balloons	
ropes, long	25	short ropes or chalk	
sand bag	31	soft bag with heavy filling	
scoops, plastic	5	empty plastic milk cartons cut in half	
scooterboards	14	skateboards (provided by children)	Spordas Megascoots™
shoe boxes (adult size)	37		
skittles	3	empty washing-up liquid bottles	
sticky tack	24, 26		
stopwatch	24, 25, 27, 37		
stopwatch or egg timer	8, 19, 20		
tabards or team bands, coloured	5, 12		
tags with Velcro® ends, coloured	20	coloured ribbon	Rip Tags™
targets	18	sheets of card, painted	Spordas Targetwall™
tennis balls	4, 6		
Velcro® balls	18	footballs	
whistle	19, 20		

Item	In lesson	Low-cost alternative	Commercial product
Items suggested for additional activities			
batting trainer or swingball			
containers, small opaque			
No Miss'Velcro® Catch Mitt (Spordas)			
Sticky Mitt™ Sticky Monster Mitt™		baseball glove or hand paddle	
Up Rite Safe Tee			

Glossary

Developmental coordination disorder

A marked impairment in the development of motor coordination that is not explainable by limited intellectual capacities and that is not a result of a physical disorder. The diagnosis can only be made if this impairment significantly interferes with academic achievement or with the activities of daily living.

Dyspraxia

An impairment or immaturity in the organisation of planned movement, with associated problems of perception and, occasionally, speech.

Figure–ground discrimination

The ability to select and focus on one item or object from amongst the mass of visual stimuli within the environment.

Form/shape constancy

The ability to recognise consistently an object or shape, even when viewed from different angles.

Hand–eye coordination

The ability to coordinate a hand movement to a visual goal.

Kinaesthetic

The sense of movement.

Perception

The process of using the senses to acquire information about the surrounding environment or situation.

Perceptual–motor

Involving the interpretation of sensory information to inform and direct motor coordination.

Proprioception

The sense of the position of parts of the body relative to each other.

Proprioceptors

Special receptors located in joints, muscles and tendons which relay the exact position of the limb or body part in relation to the rest of the body.

Sensory–motor

Involving the sensory and motor functions in the brain and their interaction with each other.

Spatial relationships

The ability to perceive the position of two or more objects in relation to each other and to the body.

Unilateral

Affecting or involving one side of the body only.

Vestibular

Relating to the sense of equilibrium and balance.

Visual closure

An area of visual perception where an object can be identified, even though its outline has been fragmented or can be seen only in part.

Visuo-spatial

Involving the visual perception of the spatial relationships of objects.

References

Addy, L M (1995) 'An evaluation of the Teodorescu perceptuo-motor handwriting programme', MA Thesis, University of York

Addy, L M (1996) 'A perceptuo-motor approach to handwriting', *British Journal of Occupational Therapy*, 59(a), pp.427–432

Addy, L M (2003) *How to Understand and Support Children with Dyspraxia*, Cambridge: LDA

Addy, L M (2004) *Speed Up: a kinaesthetic programme to develop fluent handwriting*, Cambridge: LDA

Addy, L M and Dixon G (1999) 'To label or not to label, that is the question!' *British Journal of Therapy and Rehabilitation*, Vol 5, No. 8

Black and Haskins (1996) 'Including all children in TOP play and BT TOP SPORT', *British Journal of Physical Education*, Primary PE focus, winter edition, pp.9–11

Dennison, P (1992) *Brain Gym*, Body Balance Books

Harvey, W J and Reid, G (2003) 'Attention-deficit/hyperactivity disorder: a review of research on movement skill performance and physical fitness', *Adapted Physical Activity Quarterly*, 20, pp.1–25

Henderson, S E and Sugden, D A (1992) *Movement Assessment Battery for Children*, London: Psychological Corporation

Korkman, M and Pesonen, A E (1994) 'A comparison of neuropsychological test profiles of children with attention-deficit/hyperactivity disorder and/or learning disorder', *Journal of Learning Disabilities*, 27, pp.383–392

Laszlo, J and Bairstow, P (1985) *Perceptual-motor Behaviour: developmental assessment and therapy*, London: Holt, Reinhart and Wilson

Payne, V G and Isaacs, L D (2002) *Human Motor Development: a lifespan approach* (5th edition), Mountain View, CA: Mayfield

Polatajko, H J *et al.* (1995) 'A clinical trial of the process-orientated treatment approach for children with developmental coordination disorder', *Developmental Medicine and Childhood Neurology*, 37, pp.310–319

Royeen, C and Lane, S (1991) 'Tactile processing and sensory defensiveness' in A Fisher, E Murray, and A Bundy (ed) *Sensory Integration: Theory and Practice*, Philadelphia: F A Davis

Russell, D *et al.* (2002) *Gross Motor Function Measure*, Cambridge: Cambridge University Press

Schoemaker, M, Hijlkemma, M and Kalverboer, A (1994) 'Physiotherapy for clumsy children: an evaluation study', *Developmental Medicine and Child Neurology*, 36, pp.143–155

Sherman, N W (2000) 'Tracking physical activity from childhood to adolescence', *The Journal of Physical Education*, Recreation and Dance, 71, p.10

Sims, K, *et al.* (1996) 'The remediation of clumsiness II: is kinaesthesis the answer?', *Developmental Medicine and Childhood Neurology*, 38, pp.988–997

Stagnitti, K, Raison, P and Ryan, P (1999) 'Sensory defensiveness syndrome: paediatric perspective and case study', *Australian Journal of Occupational Therapy*, 46, pp.175–187

Sugden, D and Wright, H (1998) *Motor Coordination Disorders in Children (Developmental Clinical Psychology and Psychiatry)*, California: Sage

Teodorescu, 1 and Addy, L M (1996) *Write from the Start: developing the fine-motor and perceptual skills for effective handwriting*, Cambridge: LDA

Van der Weel, F R, Van der Meer, A L H and Lee, D (1991) 'Effect of task on movement control in cerebral palsy: implications for assessment and therapy', *Developmental Medicine and Childhood Neurology*, 33, pp.419–427